"It is a tremendous privilege to wholeheartedly endorse this work by Zach Garza. Zach has lived Genesis 50:20 as God took his gaping father wound and is using it to heal many! This book is a must-read for any pastor, leader, or anyone impacted by the father wound. Read it and share it to let the healing continue!"

—JONATHAN "JP" POKLUDA, Pastor of *Harris Creek*,
Best-selling Author, Host of the *Becoming Something* Podcast

"Fatherlessness is an epidemic in our culture. Paul said in 1 Corinthians, "...though you have countless guides in Christ, you do not have many fathers." Zach Garza is a father to the fatherless. God has placed His heart inside of Zach to restore sons back to the heart of their Father. If you have met Zach, you have met the heart of God as a father. He is modeling this for us all in his family, his ministry, and his friendship."

—MICHAEL MILLER, Founder and Senior Pastor of *UPPERROOM*

"Many of the problems of our day can be traced back to the lack of a strong, healthy father figure in the home. In a world that is lacking fathers, Zach Garza stands out as an excellent father, a qualified mentor, and an inspiring visionary. This book will no doubt be an invaluable resource for those willing to engage with their relationship with their father."

—PETER K. LOUIS, Author and founder of *Braveheart Ministries*

tell me about your father

This book is set in the typeface *Athelas* designed by Veronika Burian and Jose Scaglione.

Paperback ISBN: 978-1-955546-57-7
Hardcover ISBN: 978-1-955546-60-7

A Publication of *Tall Pine Books*
119 E Center Street, Suite B4A | Warsaw, Indiana 46580
www.tallpinebooks.com

| 1 24 24 20 16 02 |

Published in the United States of America

tell
me
about
your
father

How to identify, process, and overcome the pain
in your relationship with your father.

Zachary Garza

Dedicated to all the men who have invested in me.

A father to the fatherless, a defender of widows,
is God in his holy dwelling. God sets the lonely in families,
he leads out the prisoners with singing.

PSALM 68:5-6

Contents

Part Four: Proclaim

Introduction

I BELIEVE A FEW things with all of my heart.

You can't be what you can't see. It is hard to be a godly adult if you don't know any godly adults. Most influence is caught rather than taught.

Relationships change lives. It is not good for man to be alone and, while books and sermons are helpful, nothing produces true, lasting change like life-on-life relationships.

The enemy wants to steal, kill, and destroy you. The most effective way he does so is by attacking the family with theft, loss, and destruction. If you are reading this book, it is highly likely that you have experienced one, or perhaps all three of these things.

That's not okay with me.

Have you ever thought about what you want your life to look like when you're 80 years old? What will you be like? Will you have a family? What things will you be focusing your attention on?

My desire for you is to be walking in freedom, hand-in-hand with the Lord. I want you to be surrounded by family at a dinner table full of smiles and laughter. Your kids and grandkids will be a joy to be around and everyone who knows you will say that you are blessed. My prayer is that you live out all that the Lord has for you.

The journey to becoming that person starts *today*.

You may not have had a godly role model growing up, but that doesn't mean you can't become one for others.

Your home or relationship with your father may not have been peaceful, but that doesn't mean you can't provide those things for your family.

The wounds of your past can be healed. Being the person you want to be can still happen.

The enemy wants to keep you stuck in cycles of bitterness, resentment, shame, and anger. The Lord wants to break you free.

It's your choice.

There is no better time to build up the courage to face your fears and embrace what God has for you.

As you read, you'll find 25 short chapters, sectioned into four parts. The first part, *prepare*, sets the stage and defines expectations. In it, I also hash out some of my own story. In part two, *pinpoint*, we will do just that: pinpoint the father wound in our own lives. Think of it like a diagnostics section.

The *process* laid out in part three is not an exact technical blueprint but a guide, pointing you to the steps that worked for me. In it, you'll find a mixture of spiritual and practical truths that have served me well over the years. I hope they do the same for you.

Finally, we will wrap things up with a *proclaim* section, emphasizing our need to export the healing that God has imported into us.

Be sure to check out the "tell me" sections at the end of each chapter. Pause to either write or reflect on those inquiries. Talk about them with a small group. They make a difference.

Whether you treat this book as a 25-day devotional, a four-week program, or a guide you work through over months or years, I pray it is a faithful companion as you move from pain to promise.

PART ONE

Prepare

CHAPTER 1

Setting the Stage

PICTURE KEVIN. HE'S in his twenties, just graduated college, and is nervously preparing for his first serious job interview. He rehearses the handshake, the eye contact, and practices his introduction. It's an exciting season as his entire life and career await him.

He slips into a pressed dress shirt and locates his best shoes. As he grabs his only silk tie from the closet, he stands in the mirror only to realize that he has no clue how to tie it. Suddenly his joyous anticipation is interrupted by a brutal reminder that he never had a father to show him how. With the reminder comes a fresh wave of pain that he sadly stuffs away and ignores.

Within minutes, he is back to business with a heart that's a little more calloused than it was before.

You and I know that holidays like Father's Day can be a fresh reminder of our father wound, but what do you do when you're enjoying a cup of coffee at your neighborhood Starbucks and you see a father hugging his daughter? How do you respond when you're attempting to fix a flat and are suddenly reminded that your dad never taught you how to put on a spare?

Waves of pain can find us when we least expect it and can sour even the most joyous occasions. Whether it's Kevin and his necktie or seeing a dad cheer for his child at a baseball game, these pain points can sneak up and steal our joy. For me, no matter what is going on in my life, certain experiences have a way of reminding me of my past.

Growing up without a father and the impact it continues to have on me is, without a doubt, the most difficult thing I have had to deal with in my life. Different seasons present unique issues. Various events may bring up feelings of hurt or grief. Dealing with this father wound and recognizing the impact it has on all areas of life is a marathon, not a sprint. I am now going on three decades of my father issues, and symptoms of this disease still manage to pop up. It is the unfortunate gift that keeps on giving.

I wish I could take a course and be over all of my issues. It would be nice if a six-week counseling session would do the full trick. But dealing with the fact that my father wasn't there for me is a one-step-at-a-time journey, and every mile is different.

As a child, you were supposed to have two parents, male and female, there to care for and provide for you in equal, yet different ways. But for one reason or another, your dad couldn't make that happen. You got the short end of the stick. It is not fair. It's not how it's supposed to be.

Anyone who grows up with an unhealthy relationship with their father is at a deficit. We all have wounds from that experience. The issue is extremely common, yet everyone's experience with it is unique. No two stories are the same.

And yet here's the thing: Money can't fix this. Education has little ability to cure it. Physical strength doesn't matter, nor does social status. There's also no way around it—you have to go right *through* it. Deliverance does not come through avoidance.

Now, it is easy to pull up a chair at the pity party when hearing truth like this. It is tempting for me, a grown man, to still believe that my life will always be an uphill battle because of what happened to me when I was 13. There are only two ways to go when your heart gets punched afresh by the father wound. One way leads to depression, doubt, and death, and the other leads to identity, overcoming, and life to the fullest.

If you grew up without a father around, or if you have a strained relationship with him, I know how you feel. Maybe you have never given much thought to your past. Perhaps trust issues, bitterness, and a self-reliant mentality are causing issues at work or at home. Maybe you feel insecure and fearful and are constantly wondering if you have what it takes to be successful. If so, welcome to the club. I've been here a while.

Your issues with your father may present a form of jail that is keeping you from experiencing freedom, but God wants to break you out. You were never meant to stay there. It is hard, but it's not impossible. It is a long journey of little steps, but the destination is worth it.

I invite you on this journey of dealing with your past—to face all the emotions and issues that come with the word "father." I continue to find new levels of freedom and life to the fullest in my quest for healing by allowing God to father me. I want the same for you, too. God wants to remove aloneness and heal the wounds that are keeping you from taking your place as a son or daughter in His family. He did it for me, and I believe he wants to do it for you too. I am who I am today because the Lord helped me deal with my past.

I wrote this book to help people who grew up like I did. I wrote it with the hope that it will allow people to identify the impact that growing up without a father has on their lives and to give practical tools to overcome this. I also plan to share how I not only overcame my issues but how that has propelled me into the destiny the Lord has for me. God is clear in His Word that He is *for* the fatherless. He is near to the broken-hearted and executes justice for those without a dad. He is for us, and He wants to be our Father.

If you're feeling skeptical, fearful, or uneasy, I get it. Talking about your father can twist your heart and ruffle your emotions. Because of my hurt and childhood experiences, I never liked talking about my father. I tried at all costs to avoid even thinking on the subject.

This book will stir up some emotions for you, the reader, just like it has stirred up mine, the author. It may at times leave you feeling sad, angry, hopeful, excited, and every emotion in between. It may cause grief, and that's okay. To take something out of the darkness, where most of our father issues lie, and to get it into the light can be emotionally expensive. Exposure is a grind in the short term but a gift in the long run.

Unfortunately, there is no exact how-to manual for dealing with your relationship with your father. As much as I want it to be, this book is not a precise step-by-step blueprint for your exact past and situation. What it is, however, is a set of principles and approaches that can be customized to your specific pain points and applied to your unique trauma.

Your healing is an inside job. The freedom will come from you taking a deep dive into your own soul and having enough courage to ask yourself some tough questions. Your father obviously may have hurt you, but how you navigate that hurt is best handled between you and God.

Make no mistake, there is healing available. There is wholeness. There is freedom. The Lord wants to help you heal from your past. He wants you to see yourself as He sees you, as a child who is loved no matter what, worthy of all His attention and affirmations. He wants you to become all that He has for you. The journey awaits.

I speak often about growing up without a father as it's a huge part of my story, and the Lord has used this awful reality to be a major blessing in my life. There was a time when I was terrified to let God father me. Looking back, I should have been terrified of the alternative. Fortunately, He gave me a seat at His table, and He has made a chair available for you too.

After telling my testimony in various places, I often hear someone tearfully say, "My story is so similar to yours." At that point, I get the privilege to look that person in the eyes and say, "There is freedom. Let me tell you how the Lord changed my narrative. If He did it for me, He can do it for you."

May these pages empower us to face our pains and to shed light on the ones we didn't know existed. Freedom is closer than you think.

Let's start the journey to it together.

Tell Me...

- What made you want to pick up this book?
- As you embark on this healing journey, what are some of the desires of your heart regarding your relationship with your father? What do you want to happen? What needs to be healed?

CHAPTER 2

The Father Wound

L ET'S GET OUR definitions settled upfront. What on earth do I mean when I talk about "the father wound"?

Put simply, the father wound is the pain and hurt caused when an earthly father acts in a way that is counter to that of God the Father. It can be caused by a physically or emotionally absent father, a distracted father, or a father who failed to provide a safe and loving environment for a child to grow. It can be a father who was around, but not really engaged or fully present. It can be caused by neglect, absence, abuse, control, or withholding love, blessings, and/or affirmation. The father wound is a result of the intentional or unintentional absence of love. Simply put, you feel alone, that there is no one to guide, love, or protect you.

We all have a father wound of some kind because we all have imperfect fathers. There is not one person on earth who has gone through their life without experiencing hurt from their father, no matter how great he may have been. The father wound transcends age, race, gender, or religion. It doesn't care how much money you make or the title on your business card. It is something that we all must deal with to some degree.

You may have removed yourself from qualifying for the principles in this book, thinking to yourself, *Sure, my father was not perfect but he stuck around, and my life wasn't as messed up as some other people's.*

Whether for the sake of family loyalty or through comparing our scars with others, we tend to downplay our pain in hindsight. Don't let this be you. There are varying degrees of a father wound. Some are worse than others but all are worthy of care and healing.

Given that each person is different, even two siblings can have the same father and experience the same upbringing yet have totally different father wounds. At the end of the day, this book was not written for the people with the biggest wounds or smallest, but for those with wounds period.

Dominate or Dismiss

Typically, you have two groups when referring to the father wound. One group is those who are obsessed with their father wound and use it as an excuse to not fulfill their potential. That's team "I'd be able to hold down a job or be a good husband if my father didn't hurt me."

The other group are those who deny that the actions of their father are of any importance at all. That's the "My past does not impact who I am today" group. Both views will hinder you from fulfilling your potential. One is based in pity and the other is found in ignorance at best and pride at worst. The former allows their past to dominate them, the other dismisses it altogether. Both have harmful consequences.

I have been both of those unhealthy people. I remember someone being concerned about the impact my past was having on my relationship with others. I responded, "My past has nothing to do with who I am today." I couldn't have been more wrong. The lies the enemy used against me during that season of life was, "Your past doesn't matter. You can overcome this on your own. You can prove to them that there's nothing wrong with you."

Later, I used my father wound to discourage me from taking the risks needed to grow myself into a mature adult. Fear played a huge part in keeping me from dating women, applying for jobs, or trying new things that caught my interest. Fear of rejection, failure, and embarrassment plagued me for many years. I threw myself a pity party daily as I believed the lie, "If you fail, people are going to leave you. They will make fun of you if you fail and reject you if you try. The safe place is right here. Do not put yourself out there because you don't have what it takes to succeed."

The healthy person can be found right in the middle of the two groups of unhealthy people. This person has left both ditches and finds him or herself well-balanced, in the middle of the road (see figure below for a visual). They have identified their father wound and acknowledged the impact it's had on their life. They are able to process their past through the wisdom and counsel of wise friends and counselors. They have recognized the unhealthy

DOMINATE   ACKNOWLEDGE   DISMISS

emotions their upbringing has caused and have done what they need to eliminate those feelings in a healthy way.

Another difficulty the father wound presents is that as you mature and enter seasons of life, different feelings seem to pop up and present a new set of challenges. For example, I thought I had dealt with my father wound and was free from its grip when my first child came along. But as I held my baby boy for the first time, the enemy started to speak to me. "Isn't he amazing? I wonder if your father felt the same way about you. If he did, then why did he leave you?"

Although I have gained a tremendous amount of healing from my past, moments like this happen from time to time. Each new milestone in my kid's life is one more reminder that my father wasn't present in my life. It's an odd mix of celebration for my kid's accomplishment and grief for my own loss.

It is a relational wound with one of the two most important people in your entire life. This isn't a casual chat about how Mike from eighth grade once bullied you on the playground. This is looking at the repeated actions of your father and coming to grips with the impact it had on you. It's a hard hill to climb.

You must deal with the question, "How is my father going to respond?" when thinking about processing your wound and dealing with your past. The fear of messing up the possible peace of your family comes into play. It is difficult to bring up such an emotional topic with your family in a healthy, honest, and safe way that honors instead of attacks.

To go back into your past and revisit some painful moments is one of the hardest things you (and possibly your family) will do. It is so much easier to keep those experiences and memories hidden beneath the surface where you can manage them and keep them at bay. We must remember that the enemy wants you to hold onto these emotions, so he says, "What if nothing changes?" or "Are you sure you really feel that way? I think you're overreacting. It's not that big a deal."

Societal lies like "Men don't cry" or "If you share your feelings, you're weak" also hold us hostage from confronting our father wound. This creates tension, and we as humans don't like tension. In fact, we do all that we can to relieve our lives from dealing with things that make us feel uncomfortable. We don't like things to be messy, but the Lord wants to meet you in the middle of that mess. He wants to give you grace as you sit in the tension and face the discomfort. Sometimes God needs to break you down so that He can build you back up. They're called growing pains for a reason.

Confronting your father wound will take work and it will take time. But this process will produce freedom and healing. It will be worth it—not only for you but for the people who you love and lead as well.

Tell Me...

- What is your perspective on your father wound? Do you relate to the words "dominate" or "dismiss"?
- Put yourself in your father's shoes. What is his perspective on your relationship? How would he respond to you bringing up the topic of your relationship?

CHAPTER 3

Left

I WAS 13 WHEN my father walked out the front door for good, forever changing what the word *family* meant to me. I peered out the window, watching my dad drive away while the words, "This will be better for everyone," hung in the air.

When my dad left, he took a part of my heart with him, and the piece that was left was filled with anger, fear, and shame. I pretended all was fine when all was anything but fine. The experiences that took place in my childhood are a lot for anyone to handle, much less a kid.

I saw my father from time to time, but I had a really difficult time recognizing the man who once lived with me. It seemed that everything about him changed. He had a new perspective on life, a new girlfriend, and a new apartment. He was a new man. Before long, I wanted nothing to do with him. The sight of him in his new environment left me confused and angry.

The changes began to take a toll on me. I stopped caring about school because, after all, what would happen if I failed? It's not like my dad was going to care. I quit sports because I thought, "What was the point? No one is going to show up to watch me anyway."

When the weekend came, I did anything necessary to get attention from other people. If I had to be the wild guy at the party or the punchline of the joke when hanging out with the guys, I did that to gain acceptance. More than anything, I just wanted to be wanted. I wanted people to like me. I put an unhealthy burden on my friends to be what my family should have been. If my friends didn't respond to my calls, I would freak out for fear of being alone.

For the most part, I stayed home and watched movies and television. The more time I spent alone, however, the more the enemy's lies and tricks knocked on the door of my heart. I truly felt like I had no one. No protector. No one to ask me how I was doing. I had all of these emotions with absolutely no idea what to do with them. So I stuffed them down and pretended that all was well. The hurt that came from my father, my father wound, was negatively impacting me in more ways than I could have possibly recognized at the time.

Reactions

Few topics evoke such a wide range of emotions as fathers. When asking someone about their father, three responses are typical:

The first could be joy. You might see the responder smile readily as they sing the praises of their father. They call them Daddy or Papa because, well, why wouldn't they? This man made fatherhood a top priority. He saw it as his main responsibility to provide and care for his children. Perhaps he is considered their best friend, a true family leader, and the first person to ask for help when an issue arises. He always picks up the phone when called—always has, always will. This father has taught his children how to love and be loved, how to try your hardest, and take risks. He's been there to pick up his kids when they've fallen and celebrated their every success. This dad has cried with his children and laughed with them as well. He was intentional, provided correction, encouragement, and demonstrated how to love one's spouse well.

Another reaction is indifference. You might as well be talking about Fred the mailman because this person has suppressed all emotions tied to their father. After all, it is much easier to hide difficult emotions than to deal with them. Sure, this father was around. He even came to sporting events and took the family on vacations. He made sure they had a roof over their heads, clothes on their backs, and food in their stomachs. But was he around emotionally? Did he engage their hearts? This dad rarely said he loved his children or that he was proud of them. He believed it was someone else's job to teach you how to become an adult—the school was to educate you and the church was to teach you how to love God. Awkward topics such as emotions, sex, and the "why" behind actions or decisions were never discussed. Even today, conversations stay superficial. While there is some love between this father and his children, his children regret not having a healthy father figure. They may assume he loves them, but his kids have never or rarely heard it expressed. While his children are thankful their dad provided for the family, the fact that he missed the heart is what hurts the most. After all, it's the heart that matters.

The third response is one of pure anger, sadness, or disappointment. Things get awkward fast with a serious countenance, a curt response, or phrases uttered that aren't appropriate for church. The one who asked the question can tell he has trespassed into some place he should not have gone. Maybe a joke is made to cover up the discomfort. The topic is usually changed quickly, but not before the bitterness, resentment, and grief grab the heart. This was my response for many, many years.

In my twenties, the symptoms of my father wound only got worse. I did everything to appear as manly as possible. I worked out constantly and did whatever I could to look strong on the outside to cover up for my weakness on the inside. Desperate for love and affection, I found love in the arms of any girl who would give me a second look. Any girl who gave me attention was "the one." As often as I could, I used alcohol and drugs to numb the pain and disguised it as "having a good time." I couldn't ask for help. I didn't forgive. I constantly feared the worst scenario would happen.

I spent over a decade hating my father. I couldn't celebrate my friends' good and healthy relationships with their own fathers. I could only mock them. I was quick with a sarcastic or rude remark if you started discussing your dad. I would boil over when the topic came up. My fists would ball up with rage, unable to handle the fact that I had a missing dad and my family was broken.

So, how about you? How do you respond when the topic comes up? How is your father wound affecting your life today?

Are you the businessman who is still trying to make his father proud while your wife and children are at home wondering why dad works 70 hours a week? Are you the man who gets validation by the title on your nameplate, how much you can bench press, or how much money you have in your bank account?

Have you given up and taken the easy life because you know that you don't have what it takes to succeed? Do you constantly compare yourself to others, thinking deep down that they have something you don't? Perhaps you isolate yourself, binging video games, watching sports, or hiding in a hobby?

Are you like me, the man who constantly wonders if he's enough and loveable because you didn't feel loved as a kid? Are you the new dad who is terrified to lead his family because you never had an example of what a good husband or father looked like? Are you constantly waiting for the worst to happen because that's the way that life has always gone for you?

Do you feel like you got cheated?

Whatever the emotion you feel, pay attention to it. It is your heart's way of telling you something.

So we have two choices here. We can continue to stuff our emotions away and pretend all is well. We can run the rat race and get so busy that we never have the time or margin to do true heart work. We can live life for the weekend just so that we can go play golf or day drink by the pool with buddies, keeping ourselves distracted just enough so that we don't have to peek under the hood of our hearts. We can act tough and tell others that our past doesn't have anything to do with the person we are today.

Or we can face the truth.

We can choose to revisit the topic that we have run from for so many years. We can shine a spotlight on our hearts to find out what is truly going on. Better yet, we can invite the Lord and others who love us on a journey to help us find freedom and become our best selves—our true selves, whole and healed.

I chose the latter over a decade ago, and it gave me freedom I never thought I could have. And I want you to experience the same thing.

Would it be nice if you could bless your father instead of curse him? What kind of weight would lift from your shoulders if you could replace bitterness and anger with peace and joy?

So tell me about your father. Let's talk about it and, together, we can start to heal your past and set you on a path toward becoming all that the Lord intended you to be.

Tell Me...

- Have you been abandoned at any point, either physically or emotionally?
- When the topic of "father" comes up, do you feel joy, indifference, or anger?

- Tell me about your father. Describe your experiences with him and your relationship in detail.
- What is your typical first reaction when someone starts talking about fathers?
- Is there a time when you knew that your relationship with your father was going to be different/challenging/hurtful?

CHAPTER 4

The Warm Up

I TOOK A GROUP of high school students to Colorado one summer to give them a week they would never forget. We planned a lot of fun things to do on the trip, but the highlight of the week was going to climb a 14,000-foot mountain. I called my buddy who is an experienced climber and asked him for advice on how to best prepare.

"Exercise daily the month before we get to the mountain. Drink a ton of water. Wear hiking boots with double socks."

I relayed his advice to my students and drilled this into their heads endlessly.

Everyone listened and acted accordingly...but me. And that's why when everyone else was on the top of the mountain taking pictures and hugging each other, I was sitting on a rock halfway up the mountain with a splitting headache and a blister the size of a quarter on my heel.

In order to finish the journey, you must prepare yourself for what's to come or you may get sidelined. The better you prepare, the better odds you have of finishing the journey and getting to where you want to go.

Colleges have a welcome week to get incoming freshmen adjusted to college life. Athletes have training camps to get them ready for the season, and the military readies new soldiers with boot camp.

Anyone who has ever embarked on an unknown journey knows the importance of preparation.

As I went about healing my father wound, I found six things that helped me on the journey.

1. The Lord is My Shepherd

We all need a guide on this path.

My goal is that this book helps steer you on this journey. I also hope the experiences of others can encourage you as progress is made. But no one will be able to guide you on this journey like the Lord.

One of my favorite passages in the Bible is found in John's gospel, which says, "I am the good shepherd; I know my sheep and my sheep know me. They too will listen to my voice, and there shall be one flock and one shepherd" (John 10:14, 16).

I need a good shepherd to lead me and tell me what to do and when to do it. I need His leadership to guide me. Intimacy can grow when we allow ourselves to depend on the Lord every moment of every day. I was so tired of my past rearing its ugly head on a consistent basis. It was exhausting dealing with the same issues over and over again.

Jesus is asking us to come to Him, all who are tired and weary, and He will give us rest (see Matthew 11:28). He is asking us to depend on Him, not on our own strength, to give us what we need to start the journey. This goes against all the wisdom of the world, which says to us, "You need to figure it out. You need to be strong and deal with it. It's all on you."

For me, healing my past and restoring my relationship with my father was the catalyst that led me to a deep and intimate relationship with the Lord. The journey I went on, although long and difficult, created a foundation of faithfulness that helped me grow my faith and feel a part of His family.

My prayer is that God the Father is near to you during this process. That Jesus the Good Shepherd leads you and speaks to you in a way that you can understand Him. That the Helper, the Holy Spirit, comforts and supports you. God wants your freedom and He is ready to join you on the journey, but you have to invite Him. The Lord is a gentleman; He will never enter a place unless invited first. When you feel like you are running on empty, He has everything you need to fill your tank up again.

How might you let God shepherd you? Become like a sheep. In other words, become simple, flexible, and situate yourself under His care. Stop trying to have all the answers and figure it all out. Simply graze in His pastures (His Word and prayer). As you do, being shepherded by Jesus will be as natural as breathing.

2. Know What to Expect

Have you ever traded arm punches with an eight-year-old kid with an unusually powerful punch? What about trying mild salsa that isn't so mild? Ever been jolted by a crazy serious substitute spin instructor at your gym's beginner bike class?

Few things will catch you off guard like difficulty or pain when you were expecting ease.

I'm just going to come out and say it: this isn't going to be an easy journey. It took you a while to get where you find yourself today, and it's going to take a minute to get where you want to be. I am going to share with you some issues that I faced that I didn't necessarily see coming in an effort to better prepare you for the journey.

I didn't expect other people to have such a hard time relating to what I was going through. Often when discussing issues with my dad, it was as if I was speaking a foreign language that they simply couldn't, or didn't really want to, understand. There were times when I spoke of my struggle and I was met with confusion and awkwardness. The phrases "Maybe you should just get over it" and "Enough is enough. We all have hard things happen," were spoken to me on more than one occasion. I often felt alone in the process.

I also didn't expect the hurt to be *so* deep. Once I clued into the impact my broken relationship with my father had on me, I began to see it everywhere. My identity was compromised, and I saw life through this unhealthy lens. I still say to myself, "I know my past impacted me, but does it really impact me *that* much?"

I have found the answer to be a resounding, "Yes."

Lastly, I didn't expect how much good could come out of the process. God really proved throughout this journey that He is a good Father who has good things in store for us. What the enemy meant to break me, the Lord used to build me. The harder the process, the greater the reward.

Is it hard? Yes. Would I voluntarily sign anyone up for what I went through? Not in a million years. But God has proved Himself faithful to be the healer and Father that He says He is. I never would have guessed I'd be married with children and walking in freedom doing the Lord's work, but all of that came out of processing my past.

The reason I bring this up is, as you do a deep dive into your past, I want your expectations to be on point. This is not a light self-help book but a scalpel for emotional surgery. And yes, it will hurt at times. Better to expect and embrace than to fail to plan and get stuck halfway up the mountain.

* * *

3. Find Your Team

If I need to get in shape, I call a trainer. If my tooth hurts, I get in touch with a dentist. The sink is leaking? I find a plumber. Facing your past and seeking healing isn't for the faint of heart. You're going to need to surround yourself with a team of experienced, loving people who can support you throughout this process.

Does this mean that just anyone and everyone can be on your emotional support team? Let me answer that with a question: Would you call a plumber for tooth pain?

It's important to identify those who are *qualified* to properly mentor, shepherd, and care for you along the way. There is no way that I could continue to walk in freedom without the help of friends, mentors, counselors, and pastors. They have been the ones to ask me the hard questions and to listen to me verbally process my feelings. No two mentors are the same, nor can one mentor help you with all of your issues. Each mentor is unique and has played a specific role in helping me grow in a specific area. Some mentors lasted for six weeks, while others have lasted for years. All have been so kind and patient with me as I continually dispel the lies of the enemy and strive to see myself as a son who is worthy of love.

If you are married, looping your spouse into the journey is a wise move. It is also good to have a friend or mentor around whom you can link arms with and who can fill you up when you are feeling drained. Mature pastors who are full of care and compassion can spur you along as well as support groups or church communities. If I need to deal with emotional pain, a licensed counselor may help me come to a solution. If you know a good counselor or therapist, it is rarely a bad idea to surround yourself with trained, experienced professionals who have the gift of compassion and care.

Just like climbing up a mountain alone is a bad idea, the journey will be remarkably more difficult if you try to go at it by yourself. I know it is a little intimidating to let other people in on your journey, but rarely have I met someone who doesn't want to help someone heal and experience freedom.

Your vulnerability and courage will be attractive and may even spur your friends or your group on to deal with their own past and issues. Rarely does God set you on a healing journey without letting the ripple effects impact others.

So what does this look like practically? First, identify and write out who might be on your team. You want these people to be mature, professional, and perhaps most importantly—*objective*. An immature buddy might be fun to watch a football game with, but will he stand back and objectively ask the hard questions while you open up about your past?

From there, identify the level of involvement that all parties might have in your journey. For a coed small group, they might just offer general prayer. Then, you might have a friend who you check in with once a month or so. Beyond that, you may have a pastor or counselor with whom you're meeting weekly with full transparency and open sharing.

I understand that every path is different, schedules vary, and yours might not be this formal. Regardless, finding your team is non-negotiable as you move ahead.

4. God's Timing > Our Timing

Have you ever tried to get serious about your health? It's not as easy as it sounds. Being healthy isn't something you do once and never do again. It is something you have to focus on each and every day. At first, it's hard to eat right and exercise, but after a while, it becomes second nature. Seeing progress just makes you want to double down on your efforts.

The father wound is similar in that healing takes time. There's no pill you take or magic wand you can wave to instantly overcome it. Like efforts toward health, it can be difficult at first to rewire our thinking and live with a new perspective, but over time it too becomes second nature.

For me, the process of overcoming my father wound took years of hard work and introspection. Years. That's a long time. Are there still days where I forget who I am and fall back into my old ways of thinking? Of course. But those days are few and far between. For most, the father wound is not something you *totally* get over. Meaning, old patterns of thought might try to creep back or forgiven offenses may reappear. The difference is that now you are equipped to quickly release those things and get back to center.

Think of it like this. You might pursue a journey of health that takes time. You eventually come to a point, months or years later, where you are a verifiably healthy person. It's your lifestyle now.

Does this mean you will never again be tempted with laziness? Does it mean you will never again binge-eat a sleeve of Oreos? Not necessarily. It *does* mean that these patterns are *not* your norm, and if they reappear you know how to quickly get back on track.

When I first sought healing, I became impatient and frustrated because I couldn't see what the Lord was doing. Looking back, I can see that every part of the journey had a specific purpose. Each step helped me overcome my pain and become someone who looked more and more like Jesus Christ.

We're on God's schedule and there's a reason for that. I encourage you to let the process take its time while you trust that His timing is better than ours. Some aspects might seem slow while others seem expedited. Ultimately, God is the master of the process, and we are on His schedule, not ours.

It is easy to want to take matters into your own hands and try to fast-track the healing process. You've dealt with this long enough, and you want your freedom. Unfortunately, that's not always how God works. He's more concerned about the process than the outcome. It has been said that "The man who loves the journey will walk further than the man who loves the destination."

Learn to embrace the walk. While God wants you to be free, He also wants to use this time to make you more like Him. Patience is needed, along with endurance, perseverance, and hope. All of these things are from the Lord.

God is bigger than time. He's not on anyone's schedule but His own, and time is nothing to Him. His ultimate concern is not with the speed by which you receive your freedom but with ensuring that the process is maximized to your ultimate benefit.

How long will your restoration take?

As long as it needs to.

James, the half-brother of Jesus, wrote, "Consider it pure joy, my brothers and sisters, whenever you face trials of many kinds, because you know that the testing of your faith produces perseverance. Let perseverance finish its work so that you may be mature and complete, not lacking anything" (James 1:2-4).

When we constantly watch the clock and fail to let perseverance "finish its work," we shortcut God's process. As a result, instead of being mature, complete, and lacking nothing, we are immature, incomplete, and lack much.

5. Prayer Matters

Prayer was always hard for me for several reasons. My thoughts would spiral during prayer. *Is God even listening to me? Am I doing this right? What if my heart and my words don't line up?*

When I embarked on my journey to deal with my father wound, I still had hate in my heart toward my dad and found it difficult to want good things for him. After all, he had caused me so much pain and heartache.

I confessed all this to one of my friends and he asked, "Do you pray for your father? Do you pray for your heart to change toward him?"

Honestly, that thought had never crossed my mind before. Then my friend told me about this verse, "Therefore I tell you, whatever you ask in prayer, believe that you have received it, and it will be yours" (Mark 11:24). He encouraged me to start praying for God to bless my father and for my heart to turn from hating him to having compassion on him. I took him up on that offer.

I wish I could say that all of a sudden I loved my father and wanted him to have success in all that he did. That didn't happen. But I asked the Lord to bless my father, and I sought out a new heart toward him.

I knocked on the door of change and God opened it up for me. And praying for my father day after day, month after month, and year after year did do something to my heart. As Luke 11:9 says, "And I tell you, ask, and it will be given to you; seek, and you will find; knock, and it will be opened to you." The prayers I prayed before and during this process made a massive impact on my heart.

More than just repeating a mantra or wishing for the best, I was engaging God in prayer, entreating Him to do in me what I could not do in myself.

If you've never prayed positive prayers for your father or asked God to change your heart toward him, I encourage you to start today. You'll be amazed at what the Lord can do with your earnest request.

6. Don't Quit

Referring to success, Jeffrey Fry wrote, "It's a slow process and quitting won't speed it up."

That rings true here.

The journey is hard and I can promise that you will fall during it. What matters is how you get back up. Solomon wrote, "For though the righteous fall seven times, they rise again" (Proverbs 24:16).

You will not always be able to see the progress you are making, but the freedom you will receive at the end is well worth the trials you endure to get there.

No matter what, get back up. If you don't quit, you win. This is because you have the almighty God on your side, and He's up to something even if you can't see it. He wants your freedom more than you do, and He will be right beside you every step of the way. Stay in the fight. Trust that all of this isn't in vain.

Overcoming your father wound and dealing with your past looks different for each person. So much of it depends on your background, your heart, and your season of life. What matters is not every specific method by which you deal with your wound, but that you deal with your wound.

Momentum

Just like with most things, the more you put into the process, the more you are likely to get out of it. Preparation is a necessary warm-up to the journey you are undertaking. After all, you are going into the unknown. Frankly, that can be terrifying.

Fear always pops up when you have no idea what you're about to face. The important thing to focus on is having the courage to start. Everyone who has summited Mount Everest has one thing in common: they took the first step.

It has been said that one single brick in front of a fully loaded freight train will keep that locomotive from getting started. However, if that same train is moving at just ten miles per hour, it's able to plow through a stack of bricks ten feet high and ten feet deep.

What's the difference? *Momentum.* Getting started is harder than sticking with it. So pull off the bandaid and get the difficult part over with.

Knowing what to expect and surrounding yourself with a team that loves you and is for you will help. Grasp God's timing and embrace a posture of prayer. Resolve to dismiss your instincts to quit, and you will plow through stacks of obstacles along the way.

Tell Me...

- Have you ever paid a high price for a lack of preparation? What did that look like?
- How might the truths in this chapter provide a strong mental framework for you as you go about the journey?
- During this process, the temptation to quit could be strong, especially after a hard conversation or a disappointment. What obstacles do you foresee that could pop up that might tempt you to give up?
- Following a shepherd requires us to let go of control and to be led. What are some things that you may need to let go of in order to let the Lord shepherd you?
- Any good team is made of people with different gifts and abilities. On this journey, you may need someone to encourage you, push you, and pick you up when you fall down. Who are some people who can be on your team while you prepare for this journey?

CHAPTER 5

Thinking Beyond Solo

ENGLISH POET AND preacher John Donne famously said, "No man is an island." We might all nod in agreement when reading that but what happens when we try to be that proverbial island? What's the result of isolation and missing pieces in the family unit?

Let's explore that in this chapter.

The truth is, we were made for relationships. Every single one of us, without exception, has a requirement for relationships built into our code. Most Christians understand that we were made to be connected to God on a vertical plane. However, a smaller number of people realize that we were *also* made to be connected with each other on a horizontal plane.

It's not idolatrous to say that we *need* each other. It has been that way since the beginning of time. In the garden, God provided everything that we needed.

He gave us morning so that we could work and evening so that we could rest.

He gave us land to cultivate and the seas to explore.

He gave us vegetation and fruit, crops and trees that would feed us for days and days.

He gave us animals of all shapes and sizes to join us on the Earth.

He gave us the seasons, the sun, the moon, and the stars.

Lastly, He gave man dominion over all (see Genesis 1:26).

When it was all done, He sat back and said "It is good." In fact, He looked at man and said, "It is very good."

To our surprise, God makes a U-turn a few verses later. He looks at man, who has every material thing that he could ever want: food, shelter, a place to call his own, and he assesses, "It is *not good* for man to be alone."

Until this moment everything had been good, good, good, and very good. Now, though, before sin has even entered the human race, God sees an issue: loneliness. It was not the shallow loneliness of lacking a friend but an aloneness that prevented him from sufficiently imaging the triune God and fulfilling his mandate to be fruitful and multiply.

So what does God do? He creates someone for Adam, namely, his wife, Eve. In other words, He installs a relationship in Adam's life. God is saying, "Although I have provided for your every need, you still need another human. You need someone to live life with. It's not good to be alone."

And that was the perfect life—wholeness had finally arrived. God had created the inaugural family unit. Adam had Eve, and Eve had Adam. There existed a relationship with each other and a relationship with God. God was near, ever-present, and evil was nowhere to be found in the world. There was just one, happy, peaceful *family*. Even in the Garden of Eden, where no sin was and all was perfect, a need for a network still existed.

It's clear that God's plan from the start was family. From the text, we see that family existed before the church. Family existed before governments. Family existed before markets and social clubs. Why? Because without family as the societal foundation, all of the other derivatives and offshoots will collapse. This is exactly why God's desire from the start was familial connections. In Genesis 12, God promised Abraham that all the nations of the world would be blessed through him. It was later that God expanded the promise to use Israel as a nation, but the original unit of blessing was, and is, *families*.

You were made for relationships. Yes, even you the introvert. Even you, the one who claims to not be a "people person." Even you the lone wolf. Our need for one another is inescapable.

It doesn't matter what color skin you have or where you live. It doesn't matter if you are a male or female, whether you are white collar or blue collar. It doesn't matter if you are a Republican or a Democrat. If you are rich or poor.

You were made for relationships.

And God knows this, which is why He has a plan to ensure that everyone is set up to be in relationship. He's not entering into this game without a plan, and that plan is called family.

When you were born, you automatically had two people who you were in relationship with. The Lord creates this bond between mom and dad. They fall in love, and the product of their love is you: a baby for them to care for and to call their own. That's how it's supposed to be.

God placed biological families here on Earth to be a little taste of what His family in Heaven is like.

The enemy knows this, hates it, and is bent on destroying it.

God's plan was family. Satan's plan is to destroy the family. He often starts with the father because he knows if he can take out the father, the rest will soon crumble.

The enemy wants no part of relationship, and in particular, against family. This is exactly why these close relationships can be so difficult at times. We have to understand that the enemy has come to steal your peace, kill you and your relationships, and destroy anything in this life that brings you God-given joy.

In his goal of burning relationships, he starts by lighting fires within the family. It's exactly what he did in the Garden of Eden and that is what he is doing now. If you've ever had conflict with your parents, siblings, friends, kids, or spouse, you know this to be true. Being in relationship can be difficult, and Satan wants to exploit that fact.

The enemy knows that if he can destroy your family, then he can shake the foundation of your very being. That's why family issues are at the root of so many problems.

Remember that island we talked about at the chapter's start? Satan would love to separate and surround you, leaving you to feel cut off from the rest of the pack. This can be self-imposed as adults or can be placed on us as children. The results are devastating:

- 85% of youth in prison are fatherless
- 71% of high school dropouts are fatherless
- 25% of young adults exiting Foster Care are experiencing homelessness[1]

Substance abuse, violence, and broken families wreak havoc on the souls of human beings. Consistent family conflict, divorce, and isolation are just some of the ways the enemy gets his claws into us.

God created our families to be a safe, peaceful place where we feel loved and accepted no matter what. It's no wonder things go sideways when so many of us experience the opposite of that.

If he can wound you at a young age, he doesn't have to worry about hurting you as an adult. The damage has already been done.

If your father was absent or unloving, it is hard to get the attention you need to let you know you are loved. If there was constant yelling, shouting, and chaos, living a life of security and peace could be a foreign concept to you. If no one told you they loved you, how could you believe you are worthy of love?

Life is hard, and unfortunate things happen to all of us. I think we all can agree on that. But at least if you have a healthy family, you have something of a "home base" to come back to when the storms of life hit. At least you have a team that will accept and love you no matter what. If you come from a dysfunctional family, however, you will likely be left feeling like you have nowhere to go for shelter, healing, and advice.

You were never meant to play this game of life alone, but that could be exactly how you feel: alone. No wonder life has seemed so difficult.

Some of us still have wounds from our childhood. Unless you have been intentional about healing them, they are still open and keeping you from being healthy. In many cases, we have yet to find healing from the hurts we experienced so long ago.

Those wounds have been open for long enough. It's time to take a journey to experience the healing of the Father.

Before any of that can happen, you have to come into agreement with your design. When you've been hurt by so many people for so long, it's easy to become calloused and to forgo relationships altogether.

It's a defense mechanism—a shield against being hurt. And I cannot blame you for putting it up. However, design is design. You cannot put diesel fuel in a gas engine and expect it to run well. You cannot place a man on an island by himself and expect him to run well. This defense mechanism is actually just a prison we place ourselves in. Thinking we are protecting ourselves, we are only destroying ourselves.

This prison cuts us off from the resources and riches of connections with people and causes us to miss out on the joys of doing life together. Relationship is not just some complicated mess that works for some but not for others. It is the very system that God wants us to join and flourish within.

Relationships are not just a good idea but a God idea. Without that understanding, you might not have the necessary buy-in to actually roll up your sleeves and try relationship again after being burned.

Grasping these things will bring you one step closer to mending your heart and living in the optimal design of God.

Tell Me...

- How do you feel about the word "family"? What is your first reaction or initial feeling?
- What was your childhood like? Are there any specific ways that it may have led you to self-reliance or a "solo" mentality?
- Relationships once were very hard for me. I was inauthentic, would never share my feelings, and held grudges. Evaluate your relationships. Are they difficult for you? Are there any aspects of relationships that are hard for you or that you typically avoid? What are some areas of growth you may have regarding building healthy relationships?

PART TWO

Pinpoint

CHAPTER 6

The Lies

FATHER WOUNDS ARE damaging, not merely because of the wounds but because of the lies that flow from them. If the wound itself is the prison cell, it's the lies from the enemy that act as the padlock on the door.

Satan is a one-trick pony. He really only has one approach: deception. The problem is that his one trick can be pretty darn effective. Jesus warned us of this saying, "...there is no truth in him [Satan]. When he lies, he speaks his native language, for he is a liar and the father of lies" (John 8:44). Two chapters later He reiterates, "The thief comes only to steal and kill and destroy; I have come that they may have life, and have it to the full" (John 10:10).

The very downfall of man began with a simple lie. God said not to eat the fruit yet Satan showed up to call that truth into question with a simple, "Did God really say that?"

His inquiry got Adam and Eve to doubt the goodness of God. They thought there was a chance that they were smarter than God and could better navigate this life if they were the ones calling the shots. This created division between God and man and put man at odds with each other. Needless to say, the lie was pretty effective at accomplishing his goal: to steal life and cause destruction.

It's crazy to me how, even though I know the enemy uses lies to get me off track, they still work at times. I have to be on my A-game at all times to defend myself against these schemes. One lazy or distracted moment and I could find myself believing a lie that might create a disaster in my life.

When my father left, the enemy pounced on the opportunity to fill my head with destructive lies. I believed many of them. Satan knows that if he can create division among the family, then he can isolate individuals and take them out. His lies work significantly better when the protection of a father is gone.

Satan will often attack when we are most vulnerable. Times of transition often attract darkness and lies. Perhaps you just went through a disappointment or you're simply burnt out. These are the moments where you must stay on your A-game because the enemy will work overtime to exploit your weakness.

The transition of my father out of the home certainly left me vulnerable. Probably the most pervasive lie that the enemy used during that time (and continues to use) is that I am not lovable. This lie gets served up in a bunch of different ways and in multiple environments. I believed that lie when my father left, and my mother didn't have the emotional margin to give me what I needed.

The problem with the enemy's lies is that he will partner with your circumstances to seemingly validate the lie. For instance, I believed I was unlovable. This was validated if my friends ever did something without me or forgot to give me an invite. Even now, if my wife and I don't have enough time together or quality conversations, it's tempting to revert back to that same lie.

When someone believes they are not worthy of love, it does not lead to positive things. It can force someone to believe the worst, causing them to be on the lookout for evidence that people don't love them. All of this can spiral to cynicism, skepticism, a lack of love to give others, and ultimately living with a chip on the shoulder. These things lead to shutdown and personal isolation, which is exactly what the enemy wants. It is a toxic mixture of self-doubt and hopelessness.

If you've ever wondered why it's so hard to face your difficult past, this is your clue. Is there a voice in your head saying you're worthless, a failure, and weak? Have you had a desire to heal your wounds, but for some reason you just can't seem to do it? I know why these things are hard for you because they were for me. My answer may seem simple and naive, but this is an essential insight to grasp if you are going to have a breakthrough on this journey.

Here's the simple truth: You have an enemy who wants you to stay right where you are. His full-time job is preventing your healing. He is your adversary. He is against you, and he will make this difficult. Ephesians 6:10 says, "For we do not wrestle against flesh and blood, but against the rulers, against the authorities, against the cosmic powers over this present darkness."

It is going to be difficult because he will make it difficult. Lies are the mechanism by which he pulls this off. The good news is that Paul encouraged us, "For we are not unaware of his schemes" (2 Corinthians 2:11). If we are ignorant of his schemes, we will be *susceptible* to those schemes. However, once we see the lies, we can stop them. Step one is identification. In talking with people who are on their healing journey, I have narrowed down three lies the enemy tends to use to attack.

Lie 1: Nobody Cares (Isolation)

Be sober-minded; be watchful. Your adversary the devil prowls around like a roaring lion, seeking someone to devour. (1 Peter 5:6)

My son is obsessed with nature. He especially likes watching predators take out their prey. We were recently watching a documentary about lions and how they attack zebras. It's a fairly simple strategy, really. The lion finds a group of zebras and identifies which one he wants to take out. It is usually one that is hurt or weak. They wait patiently for just the right moment. Then, when the zebra least expects it, the lion runs directly at the animal, causing it to be overcome with fear. In its fear, the animal does exactly what it is not supposed to do: run away from the pack. It finds itself alone, where the lion can easily take the zebra out.

I can relate to the zebra. The enemy finds me vulnerable as I begin to deal with the wounds of my past. He waits patiently for just the right time when I put my guard down. That's when he pounces with lies—lies which lead to fear and thoughts like, "I can't tell anyone about this. No one cares. People are going to think I'm just being weak and dramatic."

What's the result? I pretend like everything is okay, which keeps me from sharing what is really going on with my friends and community. I find myself alone, even when surrounded by people. When isolation hits, the fight is already over. The enemy has you right where he wants you, and you are never going to win a battle against him one-on-one. By trickery, he has removed you from the strength of the pack.

We must be sober-minded and on the lookout, fully aware of how he operates. For me, I know my weaknesses. I'm especially vulnerable when things don't go my way or when I perceive someone has abandoned me. I have to expect an attack from the enemy when I experience those things. It's not a time for me to sulk or let my guard down, but instead an opportunity for me to say, "I know I'm a little wounded right now. I know this is when the enemy usually attacks. Be on guard."

Is this a one-and-done experience? No. It's a consistent effort. The enemy will attempt to beat you down with consistent lies and attacks. He is relentless and won't stop until he takes you out. It is a full-time job defending yourself from him. It's easy to believe that you can't fight off these attacks, but remember, one of his goals is to get you to believe the lie that you can't. In reality, you can persevere, you can overcome, and you *can* get through this.

Lie 2: You Don't Have What it Takes (Self-Doubt)

Finally, be strong in the Lord and in the strength of his might. Put on the whole armor of God, that you may be able to stand against the schemes of the devil. (Ephesians 6:10)

Buying into the fact that I have what it takes to do what God is calling me to do is a requirement in the Christian life. Paul made this clear by saying, "God is able to bless you abundantly, so that in all things at all times, having all that you need, you will abound in every good work" (2 Corinthians 9:8).

In my life, there are a few ways the enemy causes me to believe the opposite of this passage. One of those ways is through the voices of others. I've had a number of people convey to me that I am not enough. Not smart enough. Not strong enough. Not good enough. Whether the person was saying those things on purpose or if that's the message I received, the enemy used it to make me doubt myself. I believe these lies so easily because I didn't have a father there to speak the truth over me. The enemy's voice was the most constant voice speaking to me.

The other way, and this is probably more common for me, is for people to say nothing at all. No one was there to tell me I was doing a good job or that I was on the right track. I simply had no affirmation that I was making progress. Have you ever had a moment when you made progress that you were proud of only to look around and see that no one was there to celebrate you? It's a terrible feeling.

And it's subtle moments like those that the lies of the enemy start to come. Thoughts swirl, "Am I even doing this right? Is this even working? I'm probably going to find a way to screw this up. I'm a failure."

Believing in yourself is no small matter. A person filled with self-confidence and high self-esteem is a force to be reckoned with. The enemy knows this and wants to get you to see yourself in the worst light possible. He will try to bring up past failures and hurts just to get you to focus on the negative.

"Remember that time you tried and failed? You've always quit, and you're probably going to quit this too. It's too hard. Give up."

The enemy will sing that song for as long as he is seeing re-sults. For some people, that song has worked for a long, long time. The enemy's scheme is to get you to doubt yourself which, ulti-mately, is to doubt God's ability to work in you. But they are just lies. The sooner we recognize them for what they are and are able to replace them with truth, the sooner freedom will come.

For the longest time, I thought I was dumb because I didn't do well in school. I feared that because of my insufficiency and overall unlovability, I was going to be alone forever. All of those were lies that the enemy fed to me to get me to see myself in the wrong light. Where I might not have had what it took, God did.

Lie 3: You Are Always Going to Be This Way (Hopelessness)

Hope deferred makes the heart sick, but a desire fulfilled is a tree of life. (Proverbs 13:12)

I've been on this earth for a while now and I've come to realize one undeniable truth about myself: I am a needy individual. I just am. I know men aren't supposed to need lots of attention, but I guess I'm just different. Give me all the attention. I love it when someone reaches out to me just to say hello, and I'm a sucker for a person-alized note or gift. My friends make fun of me for "going deep" in conversations too much, and I could spend hours just sitting and talking.

Coming from a home where my needs for love, attention, and affirmation weren't met, it makes sense that I am so needy.

My wife is somewhat the opposite of me. She came from an upbringing completely different than mine, which is why her needs are my opposite. She is fairly self-sufficient and doesn't always favor deep conversations. She enjoys notes and gifts, but they don't move the needle for her like they do me.

You can see how this could be an issue in our marriage. I need a lot and expect her to meet my needs. Meanwhile, my wife doesn't understand why I am so needy and feels like she can never meet my expectations. We're working through it and making progress, but it is rather difficult. Just about any married person will likely relate to persistent areas of concern.

Oftentimes, I wish I wasn't so needy. I want to change so badly, but I've had a really hard time trying to figure out how to do so. I find myself hearing the lie, "Things are always going to be this way," or "You two will never be on the same page."

It's easy to believe things will never change when you've been dealing with the same issues for years. I can totally see why people give up due to the difficulties of life. "It's always going to be like this. I can't change" is a belief that is easy to subscribe to. And that's exactly what the enemy wants you to do.

The enemy wants to destroy hope and leave you in a pit of despair. The lies that we believe can feel like bondage and like we're in prison, leaving us stuck. Some of the deceptions of the enemy I have fallen victim to in the past are:

"Why try harder when there's no way you can succeed?"

"Might as well give up. There's no use."

"It's always going to be like this, so you might as well get used to it."

If he can get you to believe things will never change, things will never change. In this, he has won.

By now in the chapter, we've settled that the enemy is going to attack *and* what that attack generally looks like. But how do we prepare for battle and keep his lies from disrupting us? The answer is simple. Bear in mind, simple doesn't always mean *easy*.

We must replace the lies of the enemy with the truth of God, and doing this takes a daily, intentional, rewiring of our brains.

God calls us to be sober-minded. He tells us in Romans 12:2, "Do not conform to the pattern of this world, but be transformed by the renewing of your mind." Remember reading that *we do not wrestle against flesh and blood* earlier? Well, the second half of that verse tells us to "put on the full armor of God, so that when evil comes, you will be able to stand your ground."

Pause for a second. Notice the verse says *when*, not *if*.

An attack from the enemy is not a possibility but a promise. So armor up. Paul mentions the belt of truth, the shield of faith, the sword of the spirit, the breastplate of righteousness, the helmet of salvation, and the sandals of peace.

Books have been written dissecting each aspect of God's armory, but for now, I'll say don't leave anything out. With intentionality, study every piece of the armor and make a conscious choice to apply these things. You can stumble into bondage but you won't stumble out. It takes an intentional stand.

We must continually renew our minds, every minute of every hour. Knowing God's Word will fill our hearts with His truth instead of being prone to believe the lies of the enemy. Other things like being joyful and focusing on what you're doing right instead of what you're doing wrong help as well. I'm not talking about unrealistic optimism but intentional optimism. We naturally want to drift toward the bad in our thoughts and focus, so it takes a lot of work to steer ourselves toward the good. I want God's perspective on how I am doing, not some other person's perspective and certainly not the enemy's.

Topics like spiritual warfare and rewiring the brain have been covered at length in many great books. While I wanted to shed light on these things, the aim of this book is not a deep dive into Christian psychology. For further reading on the topic, may I recommend: *Winning the War in Your Mind* by Craig Groeshel, *Get Out of Your Head* by Jennie Allen, as well as *Mindset* by Carol Dweck, and *Learned Optimism* by Martin Seligman. All of these books have had a profound impact on how I manage my thought life, rid my thinking of lies, and embrace freedom.

Renewing and rewiring the mind is an act of maintenance. This means it is an ongoing pursuit. Even the most sanctified saints will never graduate to a place where they no longer require the renewing of the mind. Replacing lies with truth is a life-long journey and one that is more than worthwhile.

Easy? No. Effective? More than you can imagine.

Tell Me...

- On the next pages, do the following exercise. Fill out the chart and answer "What lies do you believe?" and "What are the opposite of those lies?" An example chart is provided.

Example

LIE	TRUTH
I can't do what God has called me to do. I don't have what it takes.	I can do what the Lord has called me to do.
I am a bad husband, father, and leader.	I am a good husband, father, and leader.
I'm a Saul. I'm a fake and insecure.	I am a David, confident in God.
I'm angry, critical, and fearful.	I am a patient and gentle man who celebrates well because he trusts God.
I'm selfish and prideful. I'm a people pleaser and I'll eventually fail.	I will succeed and I care more about pleasing God than pleasing man. I want what God wants.
My family is going to be cursed because I am going to fail.	My family will be taken care of because God is a good Father who loves us and is for us.
I'm an imposter.	I'm the real deal.
I don't hear the Lord and am on my own.	I can trust the Holy Spirit inside me.
God's love is conditional and dependent upon my performance.	God's love is unconditional and not dependent on my performance.
No one really likes me.	I am surrounded by godly friends and a community who love me and are for me.

LIE	TRUTH

CHAPTER 7

My Diagnoses

I T'S PRETTY TOUGH to fix a leak you can't find. It's even harder to heal a heart wound that you haven't located.

Identifying my father wound wasn't a one-time event. It happened over the course of nearly ten years and was a multi-step process. Imagine buying a fixer-upper of a home to restore. Discovering all of the issues and problems won't happen during a one-time walk-through. Peeling back layers at a time might reveal things in disrepair that you hadn't anticipated. We know this to be true in the restoration of things like homes and cars, but how much more is this the case with the restoration of the human soul? Don't be intimidated by this. Each discovery gets you one step closer to the freedom God intended.

I realized during my journey there were two mysteries for me to solve: *Who am I, and why do I do the things I do?* Many things seemed off in my behavior. What was my motive? Was I truly comfortable being myself, or was I just a chameleon morphing into whatever others wanted me to be? I had no vision and no purpose.

I was lost. Just like Adam, I was hiding behind the fig leaves, terrified of what would happen if people saw me just as I was.

For me, there were a number of experiences that clued me into the fact that I was hurting and wounded, but the following experience stands out as a giant signal.

There aren't many things I enjoy more than going to a concert. I've always been a fan of music and have attended various concerts since junior high school. I've always been described as a "feeler," and music was a way for me to tap into my emotions. It is therapeutic in that sense.

One fall, I found out that my favorite artist was coming to town. This was going to be an incredible opportunity, not only to see my favorite band but to introduce my girlfriend to the artist as well. I immediately purchased tickets and started planning what would be the perfect night.

I bought four tickets, one for me and my girlfriend and another pair for her brother and his date. I dressed up nicely, made reservations at an amazing restaurant near the venue, and made sure we got to the concert well in advance to prepare for the show. I was beyond excited.

The concert started and immediately all of my dreams were coming true. I had a girl on my arm and was listening to my favorite artist in a beautiful venue. Does life get any better than that?

That's when my night took a turn for the worse. Two drunk frat boys sat in the empty seats in front of us.

For the next 90 minutes, these two guys talked through the entire set. They were on their phones, they complained about the songs being played and how loud it was, and they kept getting up to go to the bathroom. If they were on a mission to annoy everyone around them, they were certainly succeeding in their goal.

As the show ended, I was beginning to boil over with anger. These clowns ruined my night. They messed up my date with my girlfriend, and I wasn't able to enjoy the concert because of them.

As they left, they said something about how terrible the show was. That was when I let them have it.

I made a comment to one of them about how I didn't appreciate how they messed up the concert for me. They made a comment back. I lost my cool and grabbed one of them by the collar, threatening to punch him.

That's when my girlfriend's brother stepped in peacefully.

I'll never forget the look that he gave me. The "what's wrong with you?" look. The look on my girlfriend's face was shock and awe mixed with disappointment. I had sunk down to their level. I had behaved in an inappropriate and unacceptable manner.

Were these guys annoying? Yes. Without a doubt. But resorting to violence is something kids do, not mature adults.

I can still remember how I felt at that moment. Unable to control my emotions, I was so angry that I couldn't help but act. Right then, standing in the middle of the concert venue, I knew something was off with me. There was a wound in me, driving behavior that I could not sustain. I knew I had to take action if I wanted to become the man that I wanted to be.

Beyond almost creating an episode of Jerry Springer after the concert, I have had several other moments that helped me identify internal pain. I'd like to share some of these with you, not because of a self-indulgent desire to tell stories, but because they might act as a template for your own identification process. Figuring out that you are wounded often happens unexpectedly. You might be surprised at your own behavior in the course of your day or caught off guard by one of your own responses. As we lean into this process, we should look out for these subtle or not-so-subtle instances in order to recognize pain points.

The key is not to just spot the pain. Instead, our aim is to recognize the pain and then trace it back to its origin. Think of it like this. You plug in a massive string of lights to hang for Christmas. Upon plugging it in, you realize the bulbs are all dead. Do you leave it there? Do you walk away, satisfied that you diagnosed a problem? No, you painstakingly check each bulb for the dud so that you can fix the *root cause* and get the whole thing working again. The same goes for our recognition of the father wound. We can't just recognize *off* behavior in ourselves and leave it there. We must factor in how our upbringing is playing a role.

Unprocessed Emotion

One of the early dominos to fall in the identification process was tipped over by a man named Bob. Bob was a professor at my college and was in charge of the summer camps that I worked at. Due to my past, I often had issues with older men in leadership roles, but Bob was different. He was the first man in my life who I felt as though he didn't have an agenda for me. Bob didn't try to change my behavior or tell me all the things I was doing wrong. Instead, he seemed to enjoy being around me. A man enjoying my presence was something I had little experience with.

Over the next three years, Bob and I spent a lot of time together. Yes, he was my boss, but he was also a man whose door was always open to me. I began to trust Bob and slowly but surely allowed him to get to know the real me. With intentional questions and a lot of listening, brick-by-brick Bob began to dismantle the wall that I put up around my heart.

One day, Bob invited me to go to a Bible study that he was leading. Because I cared so much about him and what he thought of me, I agreed to go. It was at this Bible study that the Lord began to show me the impact my past was having on my life. After an icebreaker and a song or two, Bob started talking about the subject for discussion: God the Father. Pretty soon in the discussion, Bob said, "God put fathers here on earth to be an example of Him. For some of you, the actions of your father resemble the actions of God the Father. But for some of you, that's not the case."

As Bob and the group continued to discuss God the Father,

I began to feel overwhelmed with emotion. I had a lump in my throat. I started to get angry and clenched my fists. The worst part of the whole experience was that all the emotions I had been suppressing for years and years began to rise in my chest.

Before I knew it, I was crying uncontrollably and couldn't stop. It was the first time I had cried in years. Embarrassed and not knowing what to do, I got up from the devotional and left. When Bob saw me leave, he started to chase after me. When he found me, I was a mess, and in my mess, Bob grabbed me by the back of my head and pulled me in for a hug. While we were embracing, Bob said, "Zach, I love you, but you have to deal with the issues from your past because they are killing you on the inside."

It was at this moment that I first became aware that the wounds in me that were driving my behavior were not just any wound but a father wound.

I'm Not Where I Want to Be

I had a friend named Elizabeth who came from a healthy family. She lived with her parents after college and anytime she would invite me over for dinner, I would accept. I would be a fool to turn away free food.

As I sat at those dinners, surrounded by her siblings and her parents, it became painfully clear to me that I was not like these people. They asked really good questions and seemed to care about what was going on in your life. I only talked about myself.

They were constantly learning, always discussing the last book they read or the most current world event. I only watched and read about sports.

They could present their opinions on things and have civilized conversations. They even knew how to have healthy conflict, working their disagreements out by way of conversation. I typically just yelled at people or shut down.

Her parents loved each other. Elizabeth's dad built up the family and instilled self-confidence and courage into his children. The mother selflessly served and made sure everyone had what they needed.

What was this bizarro world? I had never seen anything like it, but I liked what I was experiencing. I had never been a part of a safe environment where people could flourish and thrive because of their healthy foundation of family.

What these people had was attractive. I wanted to carry myself how they carried themselves. I desired to better myself day by day through continuous learning. I wanted the healthy family that they had. You can't be what you can't see, and this family gave me a blueprint of what a healthy family, and more specifically a healthy father, looked like. It was clear to me that something was lacking. I needed to up my game if I wanted the family that I never had.

At these dinners, I was not just given food but a model. Whether they realized it or not, I was getting a taste of what was possible when family was done God's way. What I lacked in my own upbringing I saw in them, and this imparted to me an appetite for something greater.

What's the Big Deal?

I became pretty serious with a girl whom I dated off and on for a few years in my mid-twenties. This girl was a really good person, and on paper, it made sense that we should be together, but for one reason or another, it just never felt right. I knew that and she knew that, but we stayed together anyway. Eventually, we came to the point in the relationship where we were either going to get married or break up. And while I was determined to make it work, she didn't feel the same way and broke up with me.

I was crushed. I felt rejected and believed that I would never get married or find anyone who would love me. It took me a few months to regain composure, and when I did, I began to realize that I was making a huge deal out of this relationship. I know breakups are hard, but should a breakup completely sideline a grown man for months, leaving him questioning everything about his life?

This led me to ask myself some questions. For instance, "Why did you want to marry her so bad if you knew that she wasn't right for you?" and "Why did the fact that it didn't work out toss you into such a black hole for so long?" The self-reflection I was doing caused me to ask some more questions like, "Why am I so angry all the time?" and "Why do I worry so much about what people think of me?"

I was unhappy and couldn't find anything to make me feel better. I had tried all that I could think of and had come to the end of my rope. Why was I the way that I was? Why did I do the very things that I hated doing? When I looked in the mirror, I didn't like who I was. It was finally time to make a change.

Alex the Mentor

When it became apparent to me that I was not on the right path, I finally concluded that I could not do this on my own and that I needed some help.

Where would I go to get such wisdom? Elizabeth's dad seemed like a good place to start.

One evening, I built up the courage to approach and ask him for help.

"Mr. Quinn, I was wondering if you wouldn't mind grabbing coffee with me every so often to mentor me. Just help me out a little bit to teach me some things about being successful."

He looked at me and said, "Unfortunately, I don't think I can help you, Zach. But let me ask some of my friends. They may be able to meet with you."

Not the answer I was looking for, but better than nothing. A few weeks later, he introduced me to his buddy Alex. We briefly met for coffee, and I guess the way that I carried myself must have alerted him that I had issues beneath the surface. After our first meeting, Alex invited me to spend the next six Wednesday nights at his house for a few hours for the two of us to better get to know each other.

During our first meeting, Alex said, "Zach, I can see that you have issues with your father. Let's talk about that." The week after that he told me that I had an issue with holding grudges and forgiveness. The following weeks we spoke about my pride, insecurity, fear, and how all of these things were a product of my relationship with my father.

Now normally if a man who I barely knew brought up such intimate topics and pointed out the flaws I had in my life, it more than likely would not have ended well, but for some reason this was different. Because my desire to change was so great, the Lord gave me the strength and courage to confront my issues. It was during those meetings that the Lord used Alex to shine a spotlight on the things that were holding me hostage in life.

I asked him the most dangerous question you can ask someone: "What is something you see in me that I don't see that is keeping me from becoming all that I can be?"

I hid my issues in the dark recesses of my soul for a long time, and it is impossible to work on something in the dark. Only in the light can true progress be made. Asking for help and talking about my shortcomings brought my issues from the darkness into the light.

Unforgiveness. Fear. Pride. Insecurity. Many things came to light, and I was finally receiving some clarity on the steps that needed to be taken for me to experience freedom.

Pursuing older, wiser mentors gave me a covering and someone I could turn to for advice. When they told me to do something, I actually did it. A mentor's impact is limited to what you do with the advice they give.

Forgiveness

Part of my healing journey included getting more serious about my faith and investing in programs that could help solidify my spiritual foundation. One of those was a summer-long disciple-ship program in Nashville, Tennessee. This was a program de-signed to take young adults through a six-week process to help them follow Jesus with all of their hearts and become leaders in their spheres of influence.

The program consisted of about six adults leading a group of 15 through a daily curriculum of worship, study, and evangelism. One of the core teachings of this program was called *The Father Heart of God*. It was apparent from the get-go that all things father made me uncomfortable and tense. It was certainly my least favor-ite part of the ordeal.

Steve Allen, the director of the program, noticed my aversion to this topic and decided to engage me in it. Over a few weeks, Steve started asking questions to put the puzzle pieces together about my relationship with my father. He began by asking about my family, which made it clear that I had issues with my father. A few days later, he asked what I felt about my father, and he re-ceived a short response filled with anger and hurt. The next week, one of the teachings was on the role earthly fathers play in our re-lating to God the Father.

We also talked about forgiving our fathers and releasing bit-terness toward any pain that they may have caused us. He men-tioned the fact that the Lord is more than willing to wait for us to complete the "forgiveness assignment" before He gives us anoth-er one. Needless to say, I was not the most engaged during any of these discussions. Steve was wise enough to let my emotions sim-mer down before he approached me on the subject.

Later on in the program, we did another exercise called *Cre-ating Your Vision Statement*, where you go back through your past experiences to formulate what you believe your purpose is here on earth. As a forward thinker, I was all in on this exercise and couldn't wait to figure out what God had for me in my future. One of the questions to guide us through this process was, "Has there been any experience in your past that has birthed in you some kind of passion?"

I thought hard about that question and answered, "I am passionate about helping kids feel supported and loved because I didn't have that as a child." My answer cracked open the door to my heart, and Steve seized the opportunity to start my journey of healing. He knew passion often comes from pain.

The next day during worship, he came and sat next to me. He then asked me a series of questions that exposed my pain:

- What do you feel toward your father?
- How is holding onto those feelings working out for you?
- How does the Lord feel about your anger, bitterness, and unforgiveness?
- What does the Bible say about those topics?
- What are you going to do about it?

It was at that moment that I realized I needed to forgive my father. I felt like God was asking me to do so. It became less of a question of desire and more of an issue of obedience. If God was asking me to forgive my dad, would I obey Him?

My father and I had not spoken in years. I wanted to hold on to those negative feelings for a number of reasons. I was scared to confront my past, and I wanted to punish my father for what he had done. But it was at that moment that I came to the conclusion that I had two choices: Remain unforgiving toward my father or do what the Lord tells me to do and forgive him.

I chose the latter.

I had a feeling that this was the beginning of the process of overcoming my father wound. That feeling was accurate. But I didn't expect it to get worse before it got better.

Tell Me...

- Are you able to diagnose a father wound within yourself? What does that look like? How has it impacted you?
- What are some of the ways you are aware of the negative impact your father wound has had on your life? Can you recall experiences where it held you back?
- Do you have any anger, bitterness, or apathy toward your father? If so, how does that manifest in your day-to-day life?
- Can you identify a potential mentor in your life who might be able to help diagnose a father wound in your life? Who can help you see your blind spots? How can you start that conversation to ask them to help you?

CHAPTER 8

My Process

WHEN I FINALLY hit rock bottom, I was miserable and lost. I had nowhere to go and no clue what I needed. I knew who I didn't want to be, but had no vision for the man I wanted to become. I was determined to not abandon those around me like my father had—but that's a far cry from knowing who I wanted to become. Many know to run *from* the example of their fathers but they don't know how to run *to* a better one. For me, I had no friends, father figures, or sense of community. All I had was a desire to be satisfied, a desire to change.

Fortunately for me, the Lord had a plan to pick me up out of the muck and mire that I found myself in. The plan's name was Luke. I first met Luke when he came over to visit one of my roommates. He seemed like a pretty cool guy, but I was so sad and depressed that I didn't really make an effort to hang out with anyone.

One November day, I was sitting in my room sulking when Luke popped his head in. He said, "Hey, man. Some guys I know are throwing a Thanksgiving potluck dinner tonight. You should come." I politely declined his invitation when he said, "Dude. You're sitting here in a dark room in the middle of the day. You have nothing else to do. Just come." His bluntness inspired me to go.

While at this party, I made it my mission to look like I didn't want to be there. I crossed my arms, stood in the corner, and didn't smile. My plan was working until a guy named John came walking up to me. He started with the small talk, which I responded to with one-word answers. Out of nowhere, he invited me to go to a men's Bible study he was having the following week.

I gave him the standard "Let me think about it," which, for me, was a polite way to say *no*. He asked for my number and said, "I'll call you the day of with details," and that was that, or so I thought. As I continued to stand in the corner of the party alone, I thought about what just happened. For some strange unknown reason, I said to myself, "If he calls, I'll go."

Wanting the Way

Internal desires are one thing. Public desires are something else entirely. Part of the healing process is acting upon your desire to change in the presence of community. The opportunity for just that showed up when, the following Tuesday, John called me. He gave me the details of this Bible study and told me that he wanted to see me there. Having made an internal agreement with myself, I decided to check it out.

When I approached the apartment complex where the meeting was held, the desire to improve myself gave me the courage to walk up to the door and knock. I wanted more. There had to be more to life than what I was experiencing, and I was willing to search high and low for it. The door opened, and I saw something that I will never forget: men worshiping the Lord with all of their hearts.

There were guys praying for each other and singing songs of

praise. Men were confessing doubts they had and sin struggles they wanted freedom from. I even saw a guy cry. I'll be the first to admit that the whole experience was odd to me, to say the least. It's not every day you see guys saying "I love you" and crying with each other. But something in my heart acknowledged, "These guys are different. They seem happy, secure, and in love with God. They have something I want."

I surrounded myself with these guys and, for the first time in my life, I genuinely decided to pursue the Lord with my whole heart. Their hunger made me hungry. I decided to abandon the things that I used to desire. I used to want to be liked by all and be the cool kid at the party. I wanted nothing more than to appear to be a manly man and to be loved by women. After pursuing those things for a long, long time, I accepted the fact that they weren't truly satisfying me or my heart. I tried everything and it all left me yearning for more. There was only one more thing left to try. Maybe Jesus was the answer to my issues and would give me the freedom I so badly desired.

I wasn't talking about "playing church" either. I had been doing that my whole life. I was talking about truly going all in with my relationship with Jesus. Making Him the Lord of my life, while listening and obeying to whatever He asked me to do.

I knew some things about the Bible, but I never studied it for myself.

I knew it wasn't good to sin, but I never really took sin seriously.

I read all about how good God was, but I had never truly experienced His goodness.

I had no idea where to start, so I just did the best I knew how. In some way, this was me asking God to become the perfect Father that I never had.

Anytime the guys from the Bible Study did anything, I went. Presence can be a powerful thing. I showed up every Tuesday night and, most importantly, I actually obeyed what I was learning. I was still a little unsure and insecure about the whole thing, but my hunger to have what these guys had was fuel in my tank.

One Friday afternoon, I got a phone call from John, the leader of the Bible Study. "We are going on a weekend retreat at a church a few hours from here. You want to go? We leave in an hour."

Of course, I said yes.

Little did I know that would be the weekend that the Lord ignited a fire in my heart that is still burning today. Surrounded by people worshiping the Lord with all their hearts, I prayed a prayer that I will never forget.

"Lord. I want all of you. Please show me how to do that."

I experienced Father God in a new way that weekend. The best way I could describe it is that I felt like He was pursuing me. I felt like He was running after me. I could actually feel His presence in my heart. Someone gave me a word of encouragement that was spot on. The Lord met my hunger and was inviting me into more of Him.

In truth, I didn't know exactly what this looked like. Wandering into the unknown can be scary. My desire was strong, but I didn't have the tools or the training to carry out what was burning in me.

That's when my friend John Kaserman came up to me and asked a question that would change my life.

"I was praying for you during worship and felt like the Lord wanted me to ask you if you wanted me to disciple you and teach you how to follow Jesus on an intimate level. Would you be interested in that?"

This started the second step in my processing journey: a discipleship relationship.

* * *

Finding the Way

Step one was realizing I needed change, but this second step was *actualizing* that change through consistent discipleship. John and I met every Thursday morning at 5:30 am to discuss how to build intimacy in my relationship with the Lord. He taught me how to read the Bible on my own, how to interact with the Holy Spirit, and how to apply what I was learning to my life.

He helped keep me accountable in the areas that I wanted to grow in. He vulnerably shared his celebrations and struggles to help me endure and to persevere in hope. Most importantly, he taught me how to spend time with the Lord on a daily basis. He taught me how to catch my own fish and to fill my own tank so that I wouldn't be dependent on anyone else in my walk with the Lord.

The discipline of spending quality time with the Lord daily is something I am still doing today. It is the foundation of my relationship with Him. Just like with any relationship, you must prioritize time and communication if you want it to be healthy. I learned how to do that from my discipleship relationship with John.

Don't get me wrong, my friend John is a great guy, but there isn't anything special about him. He is simply a peer who said yes to helping a new follower of Jesus learn how to build a relationship with his Lord. Someone taught him how to do it, and he was just passing down what he learned to me. He simply showed up week after week and invested in me on a consistent basis. Because of his steadfastness, my life will never be the same. God fathered me through my relationship with John.

Still hungry for more of the Lord and now equipped with some tools in my tool belt from John, the Lord put me in contact with someone else who would forever change my life.

As mentioned, growing up without a father complicated my relationship with older men. They were unfamiliar and untrustworthy. Since I didn't have much contact with them, I was not used to the tone and directness most of them spoke with. I lived with my mom and most of my teachers were women, so naturally men made me uncomfortable and insecure.

On the other hand, I desperately wanted to figure out what it meant to be a man. I would watch older men closely, from a safe distance, trying to figure out how they carried themselves and handled certain situations. Being a man myself, there was a gravitational pull that led me to environments where I could observe and experience men from a distance. I was always watching, trying to figure out for myself how to be the man that I wanted to be.

From an early age, I wanted to be what my father could not be. I wanted to be a present husband and father who led a healthy family. That would be hard to do when I literally didn't know one single older man who was a present husband and father. Who would teach me what I didn't know? Who would show me how to become the man I wanted to be? Who could I emulate to become the best version of myself?

Enter Steve Allen.

Steve's presence initiated the third step in my processing journey: finding a spiritual father. A mentor shares his wisdom, but a spiritual father shares his life. Steve did just that.

Show Me the Way

I needed an older man to lead me into the next step of my processing journey. Steve's experience as a husband, father, and follower of Jesus prepared him to handle someone like me and my past. His maturity and wisdom were needed to take me where I wanted to go.

Not only did he ask the right questions to get me started on a deeper journey, but he guided and supported me along the way with his encouragement and presence.

Because of Steve, I discovered that it is always a good idea to surround yourself with someone who has been where you are trying to go. Someone with a different perspective and who is a little further along than you in this journey of life. Someone who has your best interest in mind and whose sole purpose in your relationship is to help you become who you want to be.

For a guy who didn't have a dad or a close relationship with any men growing up, Steve and his consistent encouragement and communication gave me an example of a godly man to emulate. So much more is *caught* than taught, and I caught so much just by being around Steve and watching him live a godly life. Paul's caution that "Bad company corrupts good character" also has an inverse truth. Good company builds good character. Steve certainly did so for me.

I was also able to receive more from Steve than I would from someone my own age. He rebuked and challenged me often, and I was able to take it because of my respect for him. I trusted him more than a peer because his life was proof that he knew what he was talking about. I could call him whenever I needed help. He prayed for me often and held me accountable in areas that I wanted to change. He gave me someone to confide in and allowed me to confess and process sins that I had been hiding for decades. For the first time in my life, I had a godly man in my corner who loved me unconditionally.

Finding an older, godly mentor who has qualities that you want in your own life to invest in you can be a transformative experience. If you're a young man, look for gray hair and a stable life. If you're a young lady, find a woman who fits the picture of where you want to be. Paul wrote, "...older women must train the younger women to love their husbands and their children, to live wisely and be pure..." (Titus 2:3-4). Even the Old Testament speaks to this intergenerational ministry, "He will turn the hearts of the parents to their children, and the hearts of the children to their parents" (Malachi 4:6).

If you grew up with a missing piece in your family line, like me, this mentor might not completely and entirely fill that role, but they can sure make a good substitute.

Give Me Counsel

While Steve was able to help me process and face the majority of my issues, there were some areas that he was simply not equipped to handle. There is a ton of wisdom and humility in knowing what you can and cannot do. This led me to the fourth step of my processing journey: finding a licensed counselor. The ancient biblical wisdom rings true that "in the multitude of counselors there is safety" (Proverbs 11:14).

Every so often I find myself stuck in an issue that keeps rearing its ugly head over and over again in multiple situations. These are issues that are very complicated and need the attention of an experienced professional.

Heavy psychological issues like isolation, self-reliance, and difficulty identifying and processing my emotions are not for the faint of heart. I struggled (and still do) with choosing faith over fear, and am generally on the lookout for the next way that life is going to hurt me. I was left with major abandonment and self-esteem issues that simply couldn't be worked out over a casual coffee with a mentor.

A licensed counselor gave me a safe place to process my past and to help me identify ways my past experiences are negatively affecting me and my relationships. It gave me an objective party to help provide tools to use in my fight against the lies of the enemy. It gave me some answers to the question, "Why do I do what I do when things get hard?" and helped replace some wrong thinking with right thinking. I know counseling might not be a viable option for everyone, but I do want to challenge you to consider whether or not this could be a helpful option for you.

That last point about changing your thinking is simple but expensive. Make no mistake, changing your thought life will cost you something, but it is a wise investment in your most valuable product. Coming to terms with this and carrying it out was the final step in my process.

Change My Mind

You wouldn't believe the thoughts that go through my head on a consistent basis. In my opinion, winning the war in your mind is the hardest battle you will ever fight. The lies come and they do not stop. The battle never ends. When you defeat one lie, another seems to find a way to take its place. Paul said, "...take up the shield of faith, with which you can extinguish all the flaming arrows of the evil one." Did you catch that? It's *arrows*—plural. The attacks are not a one-time occurrence.

You spend year after year hearing the same song playing in your head, and you'll find it is pretty difficult to change the record and sing a new tune. The paths have been blazed and well laid out. It may not be good for you, but at least it's familiar. When you spend decades digging ruts in your neural pathways, don't expect them to be reversed with the snap of a finger.

Changing my thinking was not something I have had to do every so often. It's not even something I have to focus on daily. It's more of an "every moment of every day" sort of battle.

Don't be intimidated by this. It's a good thing! Think of the Mona Lisa on display at the Louvre. Because of its value, it is constantly under surveillance and monitoring. It is climate-controlled, protected from harmful light, and has an anti-vibration mount that keeps it safe in the event of an earthquake. We should see our minds as valuable holy ground. We constantly monitor it to protect it from intrusive thoughts, temptations, and fiery darts that want to drag us down.

This maintenance takes intentionality and effort, but it's far less costly than staying the same and allowing our thinking to be overgrown with spiritual weeds.

The fight is worth it. When I have a moment of failing, which happens often, the trick is to get up as soon as possible. Like quicksand, I have to get out of the lie as soon as I realize I'm in danger or else it will swallow me up. Proverb 24:16 indicates that we will fall down, but the righteous get back up. The difference between those who experience change and those who stay the same is what they do in the moments that follow failure.

For me, I've always been a middle-of-the-road guy, not the sharpest knife in the drawer but not the dullest either. As a child, I always wanted to be the smartest or most talented at something. As I get older, I realize that there are a lot of smart and talented people who are coasting through life. Some are stuck or not reaching their full potential. While being smart or talented certainly helps, the most successful people that I meet are the ones who have learned how to be optimistic, resilient, and hopeful. They simply find a way to get up when they fall down. They figure out a creative way to overcome and avoid obstacles that keep them from getting what they want. They believe in themselves and in others. They operate in faith, not fear. I believe the foundation of their success starts with their mindset and perspective on life.

You don't need the most talent or raw gifting. You simply need a heart that says "yes" to the unique process God lays out before you. My process is not your prescription. You might meet with a counselor before you connect with your own Steve Allen. Maybe you are discipled, which later leads to a lasting encounter with God. The order and exact steps are not the critical issue here. The issue is yielding to the custom journey God has for you. The issue is changing your thinking from "I'm not lovable" to "I have a lot to offer and people love me." When "I'm a failure" turns into "I can do it," I promise you will increase in joy and peace. Watch your world change as your thinking does.

Tell Me...

- Have you ever thought about your "safe place"? Is there a specific person who you feel comfortable enough to help you process your journey?

- How can you engage community around you as you go through this process? Who are the friends that you can let in, and how can they intentionally help you during this journey?
- Going to church and being moral is one thing. Being discipled is another. Have you ever intentionally been discipled before? If not, who is someone that you admire that you could ask to disciple you?
- What is it that you really want at a soul level? Is it peace? Freedom? Joy? How can you get those things? Who can help?

CHAPTER 9

Forgiveness

THE MOST IMPORTANT part of my healing journey involved driving 200 miles to meet my father so that I could forgive him face-to-face. This was especially difficult because I hadn't seen him in a long time, and I didn't know how each of us would respond to the exposure of our pasts. I didn't necessarily want to meet with my father, but my mentor Steve wouldn't let me go around the obstacle standing in the middle of the path on my way to healing. The only way around is *through*.

As I held my cell phone in my hand, pacing back and forth in the front yard for what seemed like hours, I finally got the courage up to call my father. This monumental conversation went something like this.

"Dad. I'll be in San Antonio for work. Could we have lunch?"

"Sure. Just tell me when and where and I'll be there."

"Sounds good. I'll text you when I figure it out."

The whole conversation couldn't have lasted more than 90 seconds. It was anticlimactic, to say the least. As the day drew nearer, I couldn't help but get more and more anxious. The day of the meeting, while on the road, I found myself panicking at the thought of what I was about to do. The only thing that kept me from bailing on the mission was my mentor Steve who kept encouraging me to do the hard thing.

"You know what to do Zach. Do the right thing."

"I believe in you. I'll be praying for you. You can do this."

"God tells us to honor our mother and father. You are doing that. He will bless it."

As I pulled into the parking lot of the restaurant that afternoon, I sat in my car for a while just praying and asking God to help this go well. It felt like I was walking into a battle for my freedom.

As I walked into the restaurant, I saw my father, and we made small talk as we waited in line for our food. As soon as we got our food and sat down at our table, my dad said, "So what did you want to meet about?"

This was my moment. I decided to go for it.

"Well, Dad. I kinda want to know everything. I want to know about your childhood and your marriage to Mom. I want to know why you left. I want to hear it from you."

My father, a fireman by trade who grew up in inner-city Chicago in the 1950s, has never been one to share his emotions. But, for some reason, he showed me a side of him that I had never seen and have never seen since. He opened up and told me everything. I consider that alone a true miracle.

He shared about his own chaotic childhood and how no one ever taught him how to be a husband or a father. He talked about the mistakes he made and just how difficult things were between him and my mother. He talked about how our lack of relationship hurt him, but how he understands why I would feel the way I do.

As I sat there in that restaurant that day staring at my father as he lay his heart on the table, something inside of me changed.

I went from seeing my father as this jerk who intentionally hurt me and my family to seeing him as a boy who was never taught how to be a man. The Lord removed the scales from my eyes and caused me to see my father for what he was: a broken man doing the best he could with the tools he was given. He helped me to replace anger with compassion and bitterness with forgiveness. I truly meant it when I looked him in the eyes and told him, "I forgive you for all that has happened."

Everything changed that day. And it all had to do with my heart.

We know we need to forgive our father and others who hurt us, but we may not realize how often we'll need to forgive.

When we are confronted with yet another boundary crossed, we endure being disappointed yet again, or hear another insensitive comment that catches us at a vulnerable time, it starts the forgiveness process all over again. In some ways, this helps build the muscle, and it gets easier. Other times, it can send us spiraling. We ask ourselves, "Why do I have to deal with it again after I've already dealt with my past? Did my forgiveness not "take" the first time? What's wrong with me?"

We're told to leave our hurt and bitterness at the foot of the cross so that we can forgive more easily. Okay, great, I get it. Where is the foot of the cross? Is this all an imaginary exercise? Is there a tangible thing I can do to confirm forgiveness really happened?

We pray for reconciliation and restoration, but we shouldn't be surprised when actions, words, and behaviors trigger an understanding that we have more healing to do. Sometimes offenses confirm what we've always felt to be true: sometimes people don't change. This doesn't mean we haven't forgiven correctly, but that we need to set healthy boundaries and have realistic expectations.

When I forgave my father for the negative impact his actions had on my life, somewhere in the back of my mind I was expecting him to be repentant and remorseful. I pictured him getting down on his knees and, with tears in his eyes, saying, "Son, I am so sorry.

Please forgive me." That did not happen. And his subdued reaction to my offer of forgiveness produced anger and confusion that was hard to handle. I did the hard part of building up the courage and preparing my heart to forgive, but now I have to deal with this as well? That didn't seem fair to me.

How do we prepare for a lifetime of forgiving, especially when it seems we're the only ones doing the hard work?

Forgiveness is not a free pass to allow unhealthy people to continue to hurt you. Forgiveness is freeing your heart from bitterness and anger. It is not forgetting what happened. It is refusing to be bitter over what happened.

Forgiveness is not a one-time event, but a way of living. Forgiveness is not a moment; it's a posture. To consistently choose to forgive those who hurt you on a consistent basis is one of the more difficult things in life. And why does it seem those closest to you hurt you the most often? Put simply, they have the most access. Those who are positioned to love you the most are also simultaneously positioned to possibly hurt you the most.

I love my wife, and she's the most important person in my life, but I am fairly confident that I am the one who hurts her the most. We forgive each other multiple times a day when we hurt each other's feelings. It's necessary maintenance in order to have a healthy relationship.

Jesus says in Matthew 18:21-22, "Then Peter came to Him and said, 'Lord, how often shall my brother sin against me, and I forgive him? Up to seven times?' Jesus said to him, 'I do not say to you, up to seven times, but up to seventy times seven'" (NKJV).

In other words, we *always* forgive. We forgive because God forgives us. It's a choice we make. The chapter goes on to describe the dire consequences of our refusing to forgive (see Matthew 18:35).

So how do we forgive? And how often should we forgive? Here are some practical guideposts that have helped me on my journey.

Abide

Forgiveness separates our God from all the other gods of the various religions. Our God requires no sacrifice to forgive us of our sins because He gave His Son, Jesus, as the final sacrifice. His love is not contingent upon our actions but is unconditional. Our God is a forgiving God, and Jesus gives us an example of how to emulate Him. We live a lifestyle of forgiveness by living a lifestyle of abiding in God. We do this by daily being with the Father through intimate times of prayer, Scripture reading, and being in His presence.

John 5:19 says, "Jesus gave them this answer: 'Very truly I tell you, the Son can do nothing by himself; he can do only what he sees his Father doing, because whatever the Father does the Son also does.'" In Matthew 4:19, Jesus instructs, "Come and follow me." In John 8, He tells us to "abide in his word" and "If anyone keeps my word, he will never taste death." John 15 expounds further on the importance of abiding in Jesus.

We must continually be filled with the Holy Spirit and submit our thoughts and actions to Him. To walk in the Spirit is to exhibit the fruit of the Spirit, and that is something I always want to do.

When I forget to abide, it's easy to operate from my flesh instead of walking in the Spirit. When my being with the Lord is neglected, it takes me a little longer to repent when I mess up and forgive others.

How do you abide? For me, it starts with staying intentional in my relationship with God and spending time with Him. Whether it is early in the morning, on your lunch break, or whenever you have a spare moment, spend time with God. I also engage in a few spiritual disciplines, such as reading my Bible, praying, and worshiping Him through Word and song. It means giving thanks often, living in peace with those around me, and loving my God and my neighbor to the best of my ability. It helps to reject things that cause me to be cynical and negative and to embrace those things that help me stay positive and joyful. All these practices help me to abide with God, which helps me live a life of forgiveness.

Pave the Way

It makes absolutely no sense to me, but I have a difficult relationship with my mother. It has been that way since my parents divorced. I'm sure there is more here I need to process and uncover as I continue to seek restoration and healing. My father is the one who hurt me, but I have been able to fully forgive him. My mother played the role of mom and dad and did the best she could with me. But for some reason, our relationship has struggled.

So how do I honor my mother? How do I do the right thing even if I don't want to? Obedience can help pave the way for forgiveness. Out of obedience, I call my mom once a week. I invite her over to the house to spend time with the kids. I make sure she is doing well and try my best to take care of her. When I catch myself being a jerk, which I'm sad to admit is often, I apologize. I may not meet all of her expectations, and I am not the best son in the world, but I can do everything I can to honor and respect her.

When I was in the process of forgiving my father, I would go to his house every so often. Did I want to go? No. But I went to honor him because I felt it was what the Lord had for me. I believed the Lord would bless me if I did what He said. Remember, the Scripture says, "Honor your mother and father so that it will go well with you in the land" (Exodus 20:12).

It says "honor." It doesn't say you have to enjoy it. But I have found the more you honor, the easier it gets to love that person.

In the process of honoring and loving my mother, the Lord has grown my compassion for her. I believe I am closer to restoration and freedom today than I was yesterday. God is teaching me patience and to wait for His timing, not mine, even when it doesn't make sense.

If you are having a hard time forgiving your father, or find yourself with a hardened heart, ask the Lord what baby steps He wants you to take today. Maybe it's a phone call or a note. Perhaps it's a prayer. Forgiveness is a marathon, not a sprint. Start somewhere. Walking in obedience, despite what your flesh might feel, is a great place to start.

Whether we feel like it or not, walking in simple steps of obedience paves the way for forgiveness and tender-heartedness.

Find a Safe Place to Process

As long as there is still pain, there is work to be done in the journey of forgiveness. Having a safe place and trusted friends to process the past and current interactions with your father, mother, and family is key to ensuring your heart stays pointed toward Jesus. As Ephesians 5 says, we must take the hurt and pain that resides in the darkness of our hearts and bring it into the light where the Lord can heal it.

On the way home from family functions, I am grateful for the safe space my wife provides while I vent and process my feelings. I'm not looking for her to be my therapist or counselor, but I view it as confessing the true state of my heart as she helps me take it to the Lord. If I hold it all in, it stays in the darkness and becomes a poison that destroys me from the inside out.

There was a time in my life when I was vehemently opposed to sharing my feelings or going to counseling because I thought it "made me look weak" and that it wasn't what a "real man" should do. Out of fear, I tried to control the situation and prove to everyone I was stronger than whatever life tossed at me. It didn't work. In some cases, this approach only made things worse. Admitting that I needed help and accepting guidance from a professional was a humbling experience that also helped me make progress in my journey of forgiveness. It may just do the same for you, especially in complex situations that are beyond the scope of a friend or mentor.

Give Grace

Grace is the undeserved favor of God, His gift to us which keeps giving. God lavishes grace upon us day after day even though we do not deserve it. As the Lord gives us grace, so should we give grace to those who hurt us.

One prayer that helped me give grace to my father was, "Lord, give me eyes to see my father how You see him. Please give me the grace to love him just as he is, not as he should be." The Lord answered my prayer. I went from holding offense and being bitter to giving grace and forgiveness.

Our fathers are not perfect. No one is. Even the best of fathers mess up from time to time. To have healthy relationships of any kind, we need to cast off offense and replace it with grace. How can you give grace to your father today?

Repeat the Process

That's right. When through with all these steps, go back to step one and start again. If offense and pain are a cycle, forgiveness is too. Whenever disappointments of my traumatic childhood are stirred up, it usually sets me back a few days. If new hurts and disappointments arise, it can set me back even longer. So, what do I do to get back on track?

- I repeat the process. No matter how much I don't want to, I invite the Holy Spirit into the process and ask Him to help me deal with my hurt. I pray for myself and for my heart, trusting that what James 5:16 says is true: "The prayers of a righteous man are powerful and effective."
- I read Psalm 13:1-2 and pray, "How long, Lord? Will you forget me forever? How long will you hide your face from

me? How long must I wrestle with my thoughts and day after day have sorrow in my heart?" It really is okay to tell the Lord how much your heart hurts. He can handle your honesty. He's listening. And He's never shocked that you'd feel anger or frustration or hurt to this degree. So, tell Him.

- I look to the characters in the Bible who have forgiven others. Saul was trying to kill David, but David still chose to honor Saul. Joseph was sold into slavery by his brothers, sent to another country, falsely accused, and forgotten in prison. But he never allowed circumstances to cause him to doubt the goodness of God and even had compassion for the brothers who betrayed him. Jesus forgave His executioners from the cross. Stephen cried out to the Lord on behalf of the very people who were actively stoning him to death. May these, and other examples give you strength to forgive "not seven times, but seventy-seven times seven" (Matthew 18:21-22).

- I surround myself with positive people who support me in this difficult journey. I call my friends and ask them to pray for me, putting into action Matthew 18:20, which says, "For where two or three are gathered together in my name, there am I in the midst of them." These people should nudge you toward forgiveness rather than taking sides and becoming bitter on your behalf toward the offender.

- I "enter into his gates with thanksgiving and praise" as Psalm 100 instructs, which helps me fixate on things in my life that are worthy of praise. What in your life is worthy of praise? What helps you smile, even laugh? What brings you peace? When hurt is all we see, it takes a conscious effort to change our perspective to see these things. And when we do change our perspective, we can more easily and confidently confront our hurts and move toward forgiveness.

Perhaps you don't have contact with your father, or he has passed away. Maybe the person who hurt you isn't safe to be around. If this is the case, there are still things you can do to forgive without seeing them face-to-face. I've known some people who have forgiven by writing their thoughts and feelings out. This helped them process the painful feelings and events. Others made progress just by verbally processing their heart with a friend, pastor, or counselor. The gold is found in the process, not necessarily the end result of an action or a positive response from the person who hurt you.

Living a lifestyle of forgiveness is not for the faint of heart. It takes maturity to give grace, have patience to trust God for a breakthrough in His timing, and forgive those who hurt you repeatedly.

Timing is especially important, as there is a good time and a bad time to start such a process of forgiveness. Forgiving your father requires an intense amount of emotional energy, so survey your life and see if you have the capacity to handle such a task at this point in your life. This is tricky because you can also use this as an excuse to never go through with forgiveness. The longer you wait, the longer you'll be in bondage. Look at what you have coming up in life and see if you have the energy to devote what is required to be set free.

Because forgiveness is a hard and delicate task, it is wise to have someone who can help you through the process. Find someone who you trust and who is wise enough to give you sound advice. We all could use a little help from time to time, especially when we are facing a giant this big. My mentor, Steve, helped me create a plan to speak to my father. He gave me tangible steps to complete and encouraged me when things got hard. He not only focused on my actions but on my heart as well. This is a great place to start the journey of forgiveness.

I had to make some intentional choices when creating a process with my mentor to deal with my relationship with my father. I had to find my father, call him, schedule a time to meet, and drive down to see him. If I hadn't been open to doing even one of those things, my efforts could have collapsed. It is important to think about how you are going to go about forgiving your father and make time to make your desire a reality.

Be aware that your forgiveness could backfire and not be taken well by your father. Regardless of how they respond, do what you need to do to remove the bitterness and unforgiveness you've had in your heart. If I can look myself in the mirror, look the Lord in the eyes, and say, "I've done everything I can possibly think of to redeem this situation," then I can be okay with any outcome. You cannot control the response of another human being. How they deal with your actions is between them and the Lord.

Tell Me...

- Abiding with the Lord is a time for Him to fill you up so that you can receive what you need to forgive and unconditionally love those who hurt you. What changes do you need to make in your life routine to ensure you are intentionally *abiding* in God?
- What comes to mind when you hear the phrase "forgive your father"? Where are you in that process? What are some practical steps you can take?
- What was your father's childhood like? What was his relationship like with his father? What are the lies and fears that he may be operating out of?
- What would it look like to give grace to your father? To truly accept them for who they are and to try to offer unconditional love?

CHAPTER 10

The Questions

A QUESTION CAN EASILY feel like a threat. During the course of any sort of self-improvement process or journey to freedom, questions will invariably arise. Without good answers, these questions can feel threatening or induce doubt and discouragement.

As I began to identify my father wounds, forgive those who hurt me, and take action—questions popped up. Sure, I was armed with the desire to do whatever I had to do to heal. I had mentors and help. But there were still doubt-driven questions that I needed to confront along the way.

In fact, the very first question in the Bible was posed by Satan and worked solely to sow seeds of doubt in the minds of Adam and Eve. The father of lies has been sowing those same seeds of doubt in our lives ever since, as we talked about in chapter five.

As I have matured into the man that God created me to be, I've identified some questions that only show up once in a while and others that seem to show up in nearly every decision I make. In pondering them yourself, they might help you discover the "why" behind the things you pursue, the actions you take, and the words you say.

Bear in mind, not all of these lies will apply to all people. However, the end goal of all of the enemy's lies is universal: doubting yourself and doubting God.

Question One: Do I have what it takes to succeed?

No one likes failing. It's uncomfortable and gives the enemy an opportunity to toss a ton of lies your way. But when you are trying to figure out this thing called life on your own, you are going to make plenty of mistakes and experience lots of failures.

For the longest time, my mindset orbited around avoiding failure. I thought if I failed, no one would love me, which caused me to never take risks or put myself out there. I didn't believe I could succeed. I thought I was destined to be a failure, and everyone would desert me when they found out I wasn't any good.

Even for children who come from ideal homes, becoming an adult is difficult. Transition is hard to navigate, even with support and love. Children need to hear that they have what it takes to succeed in life. This encouragement helps them endure, persevere, and get back up when they fall.

When a person doesn't have that outside encouragement, they are left to question whether or not they can pull it off. Insecurity takes hold, as they are not sure they have the tools or strength to make this journey alone. The lies come, "You are too dumb to graduate or get a good job" or "Why would you even try to do that? What makes you think you'd be any good at that?" The purpose of this question is for you to doubt yourself and never try to fulfill your potential out of fear of failure.

When this happens, one of two scenarios usually play out: either the person pretends they have what it takes to succeed while being too scared to admit they need help, or they don't know what to do and they shut down to avoid trying altogether. In this, they have already determined they don't have what it takes to succeed.

I have experienced both of these scenarios. I can't tell you how many times at work, at home, or at school I neglected to ask for help because I was too prideful to admit I didn't know how to do something. I've done the opposite as well. I didn't put forth effort in college so that I would have an excuse when I failed my classes. If I tried and failed, it would be unbearable. But if I failed without ever trying, I could play it cool.

I didn't ask a girl to my senior dance because I made myself believe she wouldn't say yes. I failed to pursue promotions at work because I felt in my heart I didn't have what it took to lead a team well.

When someone has self-directed unbelief, it is a great opportunity to step in and believe *in* them and *for* them. Even if a person doesn't think they can do it, the other person's belief in them is sometimes enough for them to keep trying and moving toward success. It's been said that "to encourage someone is to open up a person's chest and to insert courage." Who is available to install courage in your heart when you lack it on your own?

Question Two:
Who is going to help me if I don't know what to do?

I have always had a little bit of a short fuse, especially on the basketball court. If someone gets under my skin, I'm prone to overreact and make a fool of myself. That's what happened in the spring of my sophomore year of high school. We were playing pick-up basketball after school when some freshman kid started running his mouth. He said something I didn't like, and I punched him in the stomach.

He left crying, we finished the game, and I didn't think much of it. That is until his cousin and his friends found me in the halls the next day.

The cousin looked like a grown man. He had a beard and muscles I didn't know a student could have. I was a skinny little punk realizing I had made a huge mistake. This guy grabbed me by the shoulders and slammed me into the lockers.

"I want you to know that I'm going to get you back for punching my cousin," he said. "Not today, but soon. I'm coming for you." And he walked away.

I didn't know what to do. I knew I was in big trouble as this guy could pound me into the ground without much effort. I couldn't turn to my friends because they were terrified of the guy, too. I couldn't tell my coaches because I'd get in trouble for punching a freshman. I had no idea what to do and no one to turn to. Fortunately, nothing serious ever came of it.

Feeling lost was a predicament that had a way of following me. For instance, it didn't take me long in my marriage to figure out that I had no idea how to be a good husband. A year in, my wife and I were left staring at each other, saying "How the heck do we do this thing called marriage?" It seemed that daily I was trying to figure out how to pursue my wife and make her feel loved and valuable. How do we handle conflict, have a healthy sex life, or plan time with the inlaws? How can we optimize our communication and compromise where needed? It was a challenge to sort through. And just when things can't get more complicated, my wife tells me that she's pregnant.

Now I have to figure out how to be a good husband and a good father? I had no idea what to do.

In every stage of life, we encounter situations where we are clueless. In a perfect world, we'd call our father or someone who's a little further down the road of life for advice. But what if we don't have that person to rely upon? We are left to face the issue on our own. There's a strange mixture of emotions when you feel such pressure to figure it out alone. Fear of the future combined with anger that it shouldn't be this way all come together to create a terrible cocktail of negative emotions.

No matter how old you are, it does not feel good to be alone. When the enemy isolates you, it is that much easier for him to attack you. The feeling of not knowing where to turn for advice can keep you from taking risks and challenging yourself. Perhaps you stick to what you know in your career, or maybe you don't venture too far away from home in regards to where you live. The "it's all on me" mentality can end the adventure of life before it ever begins.

Question Three:
Who will show me how to be an adult?

During my engagement to my wife, it hit me that I had absolutely no clue how to be an adult or husband for that matter. You have finances and friendships and taxes and time management. Then there are responsibilities, religion, romance, and relationships. And don't even get me started on car, home, and health insurance.

There is a lot involved in becoming an adult. Any of these issues, along with whatever lies the enemy is telling you, could keep you from pursuing your dreams, starting a career, or entering a marriage to begin with. The fear of failure keeps you stuck.

If a young man grows up in a home with a distracted or absent father, who is going to teach him how to become a positive and productive man? Who is going to provide the young woman all that she needs to become a self-confident adult full of worth and value?

If a person doesn't have someone older to teach them how to be an adult, they will learn it from someone, somewhere. Society and culture are more than happy to bear that burden if no one else will. Growing up without a close relationship with my father,

I learned how to be a man on my own with some help from TV and my favorite bands.

Characters in movies showed me how cool it was to be involved in crime and that drugs weren't a big deal. Rap artists instilled in me that my friends are my family and that they are the only ones I can trust. Hollywood taught me how to be a man, and the movies were not a good classroom.

Where mentors would normally fill the gap and show me what right living looked like, I was instead tutored by pop culture.

Question Four:
How can I prove to others that I'm enough?

If a child's father doesn't tell them that they are enough, they will look to the world to answer that question for them. I have seen this play out in two different ways: Either the child will prove that they are enough by achievements, or they will yield to the lie that they are not enough, and this behavior can extend well into adulthood.

For women, they may try many things to get someone else to tell them they are enough. Whether it's their boss or the guy at the end of the bar, they will figure out a way to get what they need.

For men, Jeffrey Marx and Joe Ehrmann describe the chase to prove yourself in the book *Season of Life: A Football Star, a Boy, a Journey to Manhood:*

> From the ball field to bedroom to billfold...As a young boy, I'm going to compare my athletic abilities to yours and compete for whatever attention that brings. When I get older, I'm going to compare my girlfriend to yours and compete for whatever status I can acquire by being with the prettiest or the coolest or the best girl I can get. Ultimately, as adults, we compare bank accounts and job titles, houses and cars, and we compete for the amount of security and power those represent. We will even com-

pare our children and compete for some sense of father-hood and significance attached to their achievements. We compare, we compete. That's all we do. It leaves most men feeling isolated and alone.

That was me. One of the main lies I believed as a teenager was "I don't have what it takes to succeed." For about a decade, I worked out and took a ton of weightlifting supplements to have big muscles. I did this for two reasons: to make people think I was tough and manly and to get girls to notice me. I pursued the best-looking girls and bragged to all my friends about my dating life. While I've never made a lot of money, I still to this day find it tempting to brag about the accomplishments I've achieved to make myself appear smart and successful.

For those who are on the other side of the coin, they may disappear into the shadows due to their belief that they are not enough. Maybe they distract themselves with television, computers, or movies and numb the pain with everything from video games and eating, to drugs and alcohol. Their lack of self-confidence leads to laziness, fear, and fantasy. They choose to live in complacency and apathy because this is the safe option. They figure, *no need to push my luck in trying to improve the situation.*

Question Five:
Who is going to take care of me?

This question can have two vastly different answers: I will take care of myself, or I can't do anything myself and need someone to take care of me.

As a man growing up in America, there is a belief that men don't need any help and can take care of themselves. As I grew older, I saw that I needed help and couldn't do everything on my own. But I was too scared to ask for help because of my fear of rejection. Asking for help is still extremely difficult for me, no matter how old I get.

We tend to think that taking care of ourselves means not allowing anyone to get close enough to see our actual needs. You might see this way of thinking in your life when you break off romantic relationships early to keep yourself from getting hurt by the other person. Maybe it is a fear of lack, so you hold on to what you have tightly and protect it with all your being. Whatever the case, this is a protection mechanism to prevent being hurt or experiencing pain. Your actions are saying "I've been burned once.... no way I am doing that again." But this goes contrary to our nature as humans. We are not always fine, and our survival depends on others.

Alternatively, needing someone else to take care of you at all times is unhealthy as well. I can remember not being able to function if I wasn't hanging out with my friends. I wasn't okay with being alone, so I was constantly bugging them to be over at their house or inviting them to go somewhere. This also led to always having to be in a romantic relationship. When I eventually married, this mentality resulted in always requiring time from my wife. I was suffocating those whom I loved the most because the fear of not being cared for terrified me.

The balance we are called to strike is to depend on Jesus, do what we can, and allow ourselves to lean on those He brings into our lives with healthy balance and reciprocation.

Question Six:
Why did this happen to me?

In high school, I surrounded myself with friends who had the same story as me, like Phillip. Phillip's father left about the same time mine did.

Phillip and I were inseparable. I probably spent more time at his house than at my own. While we never really talked about our dads and what happened to our families, we both knew that we shared a common bond of misfortune. Occasionally, we'd broach the topic. One of us would slyly toss out something about our situations and that would open the floodgates of venting. We really had no one else to process our hurt besides each other.

One question that we kept landing on was "Why did this happen to me?" This question causes you to doubt the goodness of God. Although the Bible says that His ways are not our ways and that He can turn ashes into beauty, those words can be hard to hear when you have experienced a lot of trauma or pain at the hands of those who were supposed to love you the most.

The worst part about this question is you will never really find out the answer. The uncertainty and lack of answers can lead to more anger and confusion. Some people can accept that they will never know the answers to some of life's biggest questions. For others, not knowing drives them mad.

Question Seven:
Where am I going to get my emotional needs met?

We each have different needs. Some people need a lot of acceptance, which happens when someone is received unconditionally, even when behavior has been imperfect. For others, they receive comfort and care through affection or physical touch. Others need to hear the words "I love you," and "I care about you." Some like to have their accomplishments recognized through appreciation while others desire affirmation of who they are, not what they've done.

In a healthy family, we get those needs met in appropriate ways. But if those needs go unmet, we often turn to this world.

My primary emotional needs are attention and encouragement. For me, I gained attention by drinking the most at a party or by getting in fights with anyone who looked at me the wrong way. I got affirmation by being the funny guy or the one who wasn't afraid to do what everyone else was afraid of doing.

Later, I tried to get my needs met by striving to be the best boyfriend (eventually, husband) possible, thinking that my efforts would lead to more attention and affirmation. I was begging someone to say, "Why, thank you so much! You're the best. Let's go spend time together, just me and you."

The chase to get your needs met often leaves you empty and wanting more. You have a relational deficit and are doing all you can to make up for the lack.

Question Eight:
Can I trust people to not leave me or hurt me?

Because of my trust issues, I would cut people off at the first sign of them hurting me. I could hold a grudge with the best of them and had no problem losing a friendship over a petty offense. My fear of abandonment created unforgiveness and bitterness and that cost me a lot of really good relationships. But I soon found myself with few friends and lots of enemies. It took me a long time to realize that my distrust was the direct result of my childhood experiences.

The pain of abandonment at the hands of your father can ultimately impact every other relationship in your life. The story your wounded heart tells goes something like this:

- If you let them in, they will get to know you.
- If they get to know you, they will discover the real you.
- If they know the real you, they could be disappointed and leave you.
- If they leave you, they will hurt you.
- You don't want to get hurt.

The past also creates a false narrative that focuses on the negatives, the "what ifs" and the worst-case scenarios. It can be a self-fulfilling prophecy and perpetuate cycles of destruction. Trust, vulnerability, and authenticity—which are the foundations of a healthy relationship—are missing. This false narrative sounds something like this:

- I was hurt by the most important person in my life.
- If my own dad hurt me and didn't stick around, why would this person?
- Surely, everyone will leave me eventually.
- I will self-protect, be guarded, and believe the worst.

But being on guard, believing the worst, and looking for the worst qualities in the other person hinders relationships. Then, when the other person leaves because we are unintentionally pushing them away, we say, "See? People always leave because I'm not lovable. I knew I couldn't trust them." This continues the cycle of a lack of grace with the shortcomings of others and creates more fear within other relationships.

Question Nine:
Why do I feel the need to be perfect?

When someone overreacts to a situation, I call it a five-hundred-dollar reaction to a five-cent problem. I have experienced this many times, but one of the most memorable was during basketball tryouts the year my father left. I viewed basketball as the one thing I excelled in. In my mind, if I excelled at something, then maybe that would give me positive attention, perhaps even from my dad.

I put so much pressure on myself to be perfect during the tryouts that, when I missed an easy layup, I punched a padded wall in frustration. Pain shot through my hand. I looked down as my hand immediately started to swell. My hand was broken. The pressure to be perfect caused me to act like a fool when I messed up. And that mistake caused me to miss the entire basketball season that year.

If you didn't receive unconditional love or acceptance upon failure, it may lead to a fear of failure. We all mess up from time to time and every human being wants to know that we are loved for who we are, not only for what we do. This signals we are "good enough" and don't have to earn acceptance or love. If someone has never entered into your mess when you failed, you may feel the need to be perfect. Shame and guilt may accompany you every time you don't meet expectations, even the unrealistic expectations you unknowingly place upon yourself. You believe the only way to be loved is to be perfect. And that is an exhausting way to live.

The antidote to this is feeling and knowing that you are enough, full stop.

Question Ten: Am I lovable?

Dovetailing off of the last question is this one. It is perhaps the biggest question of all: Am I worthy of your love? Am I still loved for who I am if I fall short or don't meet expectations? Some people will go their entire lives not knowing the answer. They fight their entire lives to feel genuine love.

As I entered into marriage, I was so excited because I thought all of my fears and doubts about not being lovable would finally disappear. Nothing could be further from the truth.

My wife tried her best to love me exactly how I wanted to be loved. She made such incredible efforts to fill up my love tank but found herself constantly falling short. It seemed like nothing she did ever made me feel the love I so desperately wanted.

After numerous conversations with many people, we came to the conclusion that I could not receive love because I didn't see myself as being lovable. My actions were sabotaging the one thing I wanted most.

As mentioned, I had a hard time receiving love due to the fact that I never felt it as a child. My mom did the best job she could in raising me. I'm sure she told me she loved me many times, but I didn't hear it and I definitely didn't feel it. To this day, I find it extremely difficult to believe that someone loves me for me and not for what I do.

Someone can be doing their best to love you and yet you still might not *feel* loved. It's as though your father wound has created a callous that not only protects you from what you perceive as "bad" but also insulates you from the good. The same shield that blocks you from pain is blocking you from love.

The job of a father is to not just love his children, but also make sure they *know* and *feel* that he loves them. Words matter, and people need to hear the words "I love you."

Question Eleven:
Does God truly love me?

I always had a hard time sitting still in church as a child. Much to the dismay of the elders, I liked to talk and enjoyed hanging out with my friends during Bible class. The same thing happened almost every Sunday—the teacher would give me a warning, the teacher would send me out of the class, and then an elder would lecture me about why my actions were unacceptable. The lectures always ended with the same sentences: "Why can't you just be more like...." This left me feeling like I wasn't good enough to be at church. And if I'm not good enough for church, then what did God think of me?

When I thought of God in Heaven looking down at me, all I could picture was this gray-haired, bearded man sitting in a massive chair, shaking his head in disappointment. How could He love me when I couldn't even sit still in church? Why on earth would He spend time with someone like me? I started to believe the enemy's lies that if only I was like other Christians, God would love me. This led to rotten fruit in my life.

The moments after I had given into sin were always the worst. I was wallowing in shame, guilt, and self-hatred. I believed this was who I was: a loser who could never get it right. It's no wonder I hated myself.

Why would a God who loves me allow me to go through what I went through? How could He say that He is a good Father when I was experiencing so much pain? If God truly did love me, it's easy to believe that all of this would have been avoided.

Truth is, the answers to these questions can reveal a great deal about your heart and what you believe about yourself. The questions you ask yourself aren't necessarily bad, but the power is in the *answers* to those questions. Are the answers to those questions negative or positive? Do they build you up or tear you down? Are you seeing yourself how God sees you when you look in the mirror, or do you see something different?

The answers directly impact your everyday life. Your heart is the wellspring of life (see Proverbs 4:20). Satan wants to use these questions and the doubts they produce to poison your heart. He wants to make sure that you see the worst version of yourself and believe nothing but lies.

At the end of the day, many of these doubt-riddled questions can be dismissed with the eternally optimistic Word of God. *Do I have what it takes to succeed?* As a matter of fact, with God on my side, I don't have what it takes to *fail*. Because frankly, even if I fall short, God will pick me up and bridge the gap.

How can I prove to others that I'm enough? Wrong question. Why would I need to prove anything to anybody, considering Jesus proved my value on the cross?

Why did this happen to me? Being the victim of trauma can set us up to live a life of victimhood if we aren't careful. In this, we ask why bad things happen to us and never even regard the good things that do. If a question does not produce life, then it's not worth dwelling on.

As you can see, many of the questions in this chapter are rooted in a negative mental framework. By renewing the mind and basking in the positivity of God's plan, these questions are no longer threats but opportunities to see God's goodness play out in our journey.

Tell Me...

- Which of the questions in this chapter do you most relate to? Name a time or an experience that caused that question to be asked.
- Many of the questions that pop up for people are related to self-doubt. What situations have caused you to doubt yourself? What is God's take on that?

PART THREE

Process

CHAPTER 11

Generational Sin

I REMEMBER THE DAY my friends found out that my dad had left. Several came up to me at school and asked what happened. I didn't really know what to say. One of my classmates demanded to pay for my lunch because his parents had told him to. It was at that moment I began to feel like a charity case because I was different. I felt shame at a time when I didn't even know what shame was. Shame became anger as I couldn't understand why God would do this to me.

If God the Father was such a good Father, then why in the world would He allow my dad to leave me? It made no sense.

As time progressed, I began to see both in Scripture and in my father's background just why these things took place.

The family was God's ideal unit to help us give and receive love in a safe and caring environment. God is all about family. He loves everything about it. The unconditional love between family members which transcends time and space is one of God's favorite things. The way a family sacrifices for each other and serves each other brings delight to the Lord.

The Lord has always been interested in family and family generations. Multiple times He refers to Himself as the God of Abraham, Isaac, and Jacob, the God of grandfather, father, and son. Scripture was clear that the Messiah, Christ Himself, was to come from the generational line of David. The twelve tribes of Judah were formed by the sons of Judah. Over a dozen times in the Bible, the Lord mentions *generations.*

While we don't usually give generational lines much thought on a daily basis, God does. Perhaps it's because time is relative to the Lord—He sees the bigger picture. His ways are higher than our ways. His plans and purposes are greater than anything we can imagine.

I didn't know this when my father left, but I came from a long line of generational sin. Alcoholism, abuse, sexual deviance, addictive behaviors, and unhealthy marriages run deep in my family line. My father continued the sins he suffered from his dad, who experienced the same from his father, generation after generation. My father didn't know how to be a father because he himself never had a good father. He couldn't give me the love and attention that I needed because no one gave him the love and attention he needed.

The Bible shows us that God cares immensely about our family tree. It says He "will by no means clear the guilty, visiting the iniquity of the fathers on the children and the children's children, to the third and the fourth generation" (Exodus 34:7). This is called generational sin, and it is alive and well today. Simply put, hurt people hurt people. If your great-grandfather, your grandfather, your uncle, and your father all struggle with the same sin, odds are you will struggle with it as well.

I know my dad had an alcoholic father who was abusive toward his mother and the rest of his family. I know how my dad, as the oldest boy, shielded his mother and other siblings from his father's rage by taking the beatings himself. I am also aware that there were various forms of abuse by my father's uncle who took care of my dad during the summer months. I learned that my father pretty much raised himself and was on his own by the age of 16. He wanted nothing to do with his family and figured he'd be better off flying solo. He and his girlfriend had a child together, and he became a dad at the age of 18.

It is easy to paint the picture that my father is a terrible person. But I don't think he is. My father is a hurt person doing the best he knows how to do. He got a bad hand in this game of life, and he's simply trying to play it the best way he knows how. There is no doubt in my mind that my dad wants to be a good father. He just lacks the tools needed to engage his children at the heart level. You can't give away what you yourself don't have, and my dad got very little instruction, guidance, or love from his own father.

Gaining an understanding of generational sin will actually position you to have mercy where you didn't before. Knowing the *why* behind someone's actions can make the *what* seem less egregious. Does it excuse sinful behavior? No. But does it make it easier to give grace and forgive because you are a little more understanding of the backstory? I think so.

My father was impacted by the sins of his father and the sins of his father's father. He learned from the people he spent the most time around. We all do. The nature vs. nurture debate could go on forever, but at the end of the day, we can all agree that where we come from truly matters. Your forefathers and the generations that have come before you matter. Family matters. If not to you, it most definitely does to God.

When I first stumbled upon the topic of generational sin, I thought it was the craziest thing I had ever heard. "How in the world could things my father and grandfather did impact me? It's not like sin gets passed down through your genes like hair loss or eye color." This was my thought process. That's when someone broke it down clearly for me.

"If your granddad went to prison and so did your dad, uncle, and brother, do you think the odds are high that you'd go to prison?"

I slowly and skeptically nodded my head, "I guess that makes sense..."

"Okay. What would you say if I told you every person in your family went to college? Would you say that you would be likely to attend college?"

"Well yeah..." I said.

"You see, that's how generational sin and blessing works. If everyone in your generational line deals with an issue, whether it's poverty, alcoholism, or a short temper, odds are you will deal with that issue in one way or another. The same thing goes for the good stuff. If everyone has a healthy marriage, is well educated, and stays relatively free from vices, I'm sure the odds are pretty good you'll follow in their footsteps."

He was on to something. My experiences since that conversation have proved him to be right. Obviously, this isn't 100% true in all situations, but it does ring true and studies bear that out. For instance, the child of an alcoholic is 300% more likely to develop alcoholism as an adult, compared to children who did not have alcoholic parents.[2]

This much I know to be true: Our original parents, Adam and Eve, messed things up from the start. Since then, all of mankind has been dealing with a sort of generational sin. Some families' sins are really obvious, like alcoholism, abuse, or divorce, while other families may deal with the hidden sins of judgmentalism, pride, and greed. This gets passed down because it is in our physical and spiritual DNA, but also because it is the environment that we were born into. If all we have known is chaos and dysfunction, it makes a lot of sense that we would recreate what we know.

If it seems like finding freedom is an uphill battle, that's probably because it is. Generational sin proves to you that you are not fighting a fair fight. For me, it was disheartening to know that the odds were stacked against me, but comforting to know that I wasn't crazy for wondering why the fight was so hard.

When I realized the generational sins of my father, it was sobering. My past has, and continues to, impact who I am today. I knew then that I would become just like my father and grandfather if something didn't change. You might not intentionally sign up to inherit a generational pattern of behavior, but you *will* have to intentionally unsubscribe.

Breaking a generational sin and turning it into a generational blessing takes a lot of hard work and determination, but it could also mean freedom for your children and your children's children. You may know what it is like to have an absent or inattentive father, but your kids don't have to know what that feels like. Knowing that you are fighting for someone else makes the fight a little more bearable.

The truth is, our minds are drawn to the easy route and breaking cycles ain't easy. You need the want-to, the know-how, and the follow-through. What does the follow-through look like? You need a plan or blueprint for what life will look like on the other side of the cycle breaking.

Psychology Today published a piece that dealt with this very topic. The author notes that after breaking old cycles, you have to shift to new patterns. As you do, the learning curve can be steep, and involves answering questions like:

- What does shifting this pattern look like?
- What kind of pushback should I expect to receive?
- What are the hardest parts of changing this pattern?
- What skills do I need to learn?
- What do I need to do when I suffer a setback?[3]

It's been said that failing to plan is planning to fail. Generational sin is not removed by accident but through intentionality. Before you remove an old pattern, know in your mind, and even on paper, what you are going to replace those patterns with.

Generational blessing is the Welcome Week your first week of college, preparing you to succeed. It is the how-to manual on fulfilling your potential. The intentional job training that sets you up for success. Whenever you don't have that generational blessing, you are left to figure out life on your own. It's extremely daunting, and every day, week, and month that goes by, I find myself not knowing what to do. Because the truth is, I don't know what to do. I don't know how to be a godly man. I don't know how to be a good husband or lead my family. But just because I don't know doesn't mean I can't figure it out. I can create it. It will be one of the hardest things I've ever done, but the Lord is with me. And He's with you too.

God says in Psalm 68 that He is a Father to the fatherless. That is great news for us who feel like they are missing out on a father.

God will lead you. He will father you. You will stumble through it. You will not get everything right. But you are laying the foundation for generations to come. You might not have had a generational blessing. But you, through grit, endurance, and perseverance, can create one for your future family.

My grandkids and great-grandchildren will be different because of the work I am doing to heal my father wound. They will have a different story than I have, and it's all because Father God decided to turn my generational curse into a blessing.

But here's the question: Can you receive the blessing? For me, receiving has always been hard because receiving something that I did not earn has always been difficult. It takes a level of humility to be fathered. To be led.

It will all be worth it. Because of your hard work in dealing with your past, you could help your future generations avoid the pain and heartache that you experienced. That sounds like the best gift you could possibly give them.

Tell Me...

- Can you spot generational sin in your family line? How is it impacting you today? What is compelling you to break the cycle?
- Have you ever heard of a Genogram before? It's similar to a family tree, but with important events that impact generational lines. If not, I'd highly recommend doing some research and completing one yourself. My eyes were opened up when I saw on paper the pains of my family.
- What does Psalm 68:5 mean to you? What are some ways that God has fathered you in the past? What are some areas you need Him to father you in the future?
- Do you find it hard to receive guidance, blessing, or wisdom? If so, why may that be?

CHAPTER 12

Implications in Adulthood

THE LORD HAS called me to become what I never had: to be a father to the fatherless. He has opened doors I didn't even know existed and introduced me to people I never thought I'd meet personally. I believe this call will come to fruition through mentoring relationships, which is why I have given my life to mentoring people. Very few things bring me as much joy as seeing a young person being mentored in the name of Jesus, and it is my joy to try to make as many of those relationships happen as possible.

Yet even in the midst of this calling and joy, I still am working through my father wound. I had an incredible opportunity to interview for a new job a few years ago. This position would have given me the experience and resume that I was looking for to get to where I wanted to be. The job description fit me perfectly. The interview couldn't have gone any better. I felt peace. It looked as if this opportunity might come to fruition. But as I drove home, the first thing that popped into my mind was doubt. "Am I making the right decision? What if I fail in this new role? What if my current organization crumbles? My kids will suffer. My wife will suffer. People will laugh at me."

This wasn't a casual fleeting doubt. It hit me hard, and I pulled off the highway to compose myself. Doubt turned into fear. Fear turned into anxiety. I needed help. I called a couple of mentors, but no one answered. I called some of my friends, but no one picked up. I was searching, and I needed a guide. For the first time in a long time, I thought of how it sure would be nice to call my father right now. There was no anger attached to the thought, no animosity, but a mixture of grief, sadness, and jealousy.

There is a part of me that thinks I should be over my father wound by now. When an issue comes up that is related to growing up without a father, I sometimes say to myself, "This again? When am I going to be done with this?"

It is somewhat easy to see how growing up without a father impacts children. Typical symptoms such as anger, inability to trust, and insecurity are fairly easy to identify in children. But how does it play out into adulthood? I believe the symptoms are a little bit trickier to identify as grown-ups.

A scheme of the enemy is to keep me focused on all the ways my childhood is holding me back, but that type of negativity will only keep me spinning my wheels. There is some good that has come from my childhood. It takes work to see it, but the Lord is a God of redemption. Nothing, including my traumatic childhood, is too much for God to handle. If He truly works *all things* for our good, why would growing up without a father be any different?

I am going to be vulnerable with you right now as we discuss ways a father wound can impact us as adults. This may seem a little dark and depressing, and it is, as sin has a way of ruining whatever it touches. For those reading who aren't married or a parent, may this be a warning sign for possible obstacles in your future. I also want you to know that you're not alone should you see yourself in these areas. And we will find out how the Lord redeemed all of this in the next chapter, so hope is on the way.

Critical and Controlling Nature

We were about a decade into our marriage, and all seemed like it was going well. My wife and I had three beautiful children, my ministry was growing and expanding, and we had friends and a church body to call home. That's when my wife started experiencing pretty extreme anxiety and depression.

We tried to do whatever we could think of to try to get my wife back to her old self. We tried counseling and mentors. We changed churches and switched up our friend groups. We even ditched the fast-paced life of Dallas and moved to the smaller town of Waco, Texas. Nothing we did seemed to work.

One day, my wife and I got into a pretty big argument. I was running low on grace and compassion and let her know how frustrated I was with her outlook on life. It was not my finest moment. That's when my wife let me have it.

"All you do is focus on what I'm doing wrong. You are so quick to point out ways I could improve and how things can get better, but you never tell me the good things I am doing and you sure don't encourage me. It's hard to have good self-confidence and self-esteem when all I hear all day is what I'm doing wrong."

I was taken aback by this. To me, it seemed like she was blaming me for all of her issues. This seemed like she wasn't taking responsibility, which didn't seem fair. I had all of the reasons in the world why I wasn't the issue.

Yet she was right.

After doing some soul-searching and talking to a lot of mentors, friends, and counselors, I realized that I was being overly critical of my wife due to the big fears that I was experiencing in my own life. I started to notice some phrases that I was saying often.

"Why do you do it like that? You should do it like this."

"Don't do that. It's not going to make anything better."

"Stop it. Don't act like that, don't say that."

It didn't take long for me to see that I was using my words and my tone to control my wife's actions. Fear led to criticism and criticism led to control. The words weren't the worst part. It was the *tone* and look I gave when I said it. My wife would later say that anytime I corrected her my look and tone made her feel like a total idiot. Short, authoritative commands said in an extremely direct and critical manner do not help your wife to feel good about herself.

I zeroed in on the status of my heart and came to this conclusion.

I had a tough childhood and an absent father. More than anything, I wanted my children to have the perfect childhood. I was fearful that, if my wife said or did the wrong thing, it was going to lead to my greatest fear, which was my kids having a bad childhood. So I shut my wife down with my critical remarks and took control of the situation. I made sure she said and did the right thing. I operated with a closed fist instead of an open hand.

All of this came out of the fear of protecting my kids from having the childhood that I did. While my motives were not necessarily bad, the manifestation of those motives was skewed.

Self-confidence at Work

As a natural visionary, I love thinking about what is next. I am one of those guys who can tell you exactly what I am going to do in five years but have no idea what I'm going to do tomorrow.

When I was in my late twenties, the Lord moved my heart to start a mentoring organization. I had no idea what I was doing, but God surrounded me with great people who helped me figure it out. For five years, I worked as a teacher and a coach and built a mentoring non-profit on the side. I had no dreams of this becoming my full-time job. I simply wanted to help kids who grew up like I did.

One day, my board chairman got me a meeting with a large church in the Dallas area. The agenda was centered around whether this church would support us, which would provide more volunteers and funding. I went into my spiel about how our mentoring organization came about and where we were. I really tried to sell them on us and get on their good side, as I badly wanted their partnership. I probably spoke about 90% of the time, which is never a good sign.

As the meeting ended, the church leadership said something to the effect of, "You guys aren't ready yet. You don't even have someone on full-time staff." While this was the truth, it was hard to hear. It was like someone took my hopes and beat them over the head with a baseball bat. As the church leaders left and it was just me and my board of directors, my chairman looked at me and said something that would change my life.

"Zach," he said, "the time has come for us to hire a full-time executive director to take this organization to the next level."

"I hear you," I replied. "But who could we find to be our executive director?"

He laughed. "Zach, it's you."

I literally never thought in a million years that I could do such a thing. Growing up without a father caused me to believe I couldn't overcome obstacles. I didn't believe I had what it took to succeed and never considered what a new reality for me would look like.

Over the last decade, the Lord has put me in situation after situation where I didn't believe I could succeed. Here's a list off the top of my head:

- Networking: I didn't believe I could network because I didn't think people would want to hang out with me.
- Make phone calls: I have a stutter, and I would do anything

to avoid phone calls. This isn't a big issue unless your job involves a ton of calling people on the phone.

- Fundraising: Me? Ask people for money? Are you serious? This was about the most terrifying thing I had ever heard of.
- Be detail-oriented: As a visionary, I had a really hard time managing the day-to-day tasks that needed to be done to advance our organization. Not only was I not good at it, but I didn't like it.
- Manage a staff: I saw managing a staff as hand-holding people who weren't as hardworking as I was. I didn't like to have meetings to clarify objectives and action plans, and I didn't enjoy encouraging staff during hard times.

It is typical for me to think I am doing worse than I am. I routinely ask my board of directors if it's time to find someone else for this job. I ask permission more often than I need to out of my insecurity, and I look for someone else to make the hard decisions so that I am not responsible for the consequences. I have a hard time working in teams because I am so used to being in control and doing everything myself. These fears and actions stem from my childhood and lack of a father figure in my life. The lies of the enemy imprisoned me and kept me from dreaming or fulfilling my potential.

Dating and Marriage

As a single man, all I wanted was to get married. I can look back now and say that my desire for marriage was more about receiving love and not being alone than loving and serving someone else. Due to my upbringing, all I wanted was to be loved, and I would do whatever it took to make that happen in my dating relationships.

On the outside, this looked like I was a great boyfriend. But all my actions were selfish. If you liked flowers, and flowers got you to date me, I'd give you a dozen roses each week. If it was a man with strong faith you wanted, I would raise my hands during worship and attend every Bible study I could find. I made the other person my god and looked to them to fulfill my needs, and I was completely unaware that I was doing this.

I continued this way of thinking into my marriage. I looked to my wife to meet my needs. This sounded good in my head, but the bad news is that my wife is human and she can't measure up to these unrealistic expectations. During our first years of marriage, I said over and over, "You don't love me enough." Nothing my wife did was enough. Even when she did try to love me, I couldn't receive it. If she wrote me a love note, I would be mad she didn't give them to me more often. If she tried to give me a gift, I would pout because it wasn't the right one. The weight of my demands and the shame of hearing she was not loving me the "right way" was too much for her to handle.

I needed so much attention from her that I kept her from spending time by herself, which is the one thing my introverted wife needed the most. If she wanted to rest one night, I would see it as her not giving me love and being selfish. If it sounds like I was acting like a child, that's because I was. Due to trust issues, I held grudges, sometimes for weeks. I withheld my love and attention when she didn't meet my expectations. I gave her the silent treatment often. My immaturity caused me to act in a way that denied me the thing I wanted the most.

Because I felt unloved as a child, this produced a man who made it his mission to receive love. But here's the catch: No love from a person can fix me. I kept looking to my wife to give me something no human is capable of producing. I wanted her to be the answer to my problem, and that produced shame and guilt in the heart of my wife. All the while, the enemy was saying, "You're unlovable. No one is going to love you."

My Parenting

I've always wanted to be a dad. I wanted to be a good father and dreamed of having a healthy family of my own. I wanted to create the ideal childhood for my own children. To give them the father and the childhood that I never had.

Once I got married, I could not wait to have kids. When we had our first son, I made being a good father the top of my priority list. I read all the books on how to set my kid up for the brightest future possible. But the underlying motivation was the fear that I would somehow mess up and give my kids the same childhood I had.

What was the result? I became a helicopter dad, always hovering over my kids to make sure they were safe, productive, and set up for success. If my kid did something dangerous, I would over-react—not because I cared about their safety, but because I cared about not failing as a parent. I read books because I was scared I was missing something as a dad. I stayed up nights worrying about their education, their diet, and how much TV they watched.

I got onto them about each and every little thing to ensure that they would become all that they were intended to be. Just like in my marriage, my critical nature and controlling tendencies made my kids feel like I cared more about their behavior and their actions than their hearts.

Out of fear, I did my best to control everything I could about their lives. Yes, there is some wisdom in choosing what your child watches and what school they go to, but I knew that my motive in this was based on fear, not wisdom. I was trying to be their god, protecting them from anything that may not produce their best life. I carried the weight of their success instead of trusting it to the Lord.

That kind of weight gets heavy after a while. The fear that this responsibility breeds can cause you to elevate your children above all else, including your spouse and marriage.

Perhaps a big reason for all these fears is the fact that I felt like I was flying solo. I had people to ask, but I had an issue trusting the advice of others and letting them into my life.

As a Friend

I am a people person, an extrovert who has never met a stranger. I love being around others. But what happens when you look to others to complete you? Is it a good thing to look to others to make you happy?

Growing up with an absent father and a mother who worked all the time, my friends became my family. I relied on them for everything, and I carried that same mindset into adulthood. I took no responsibility for my own actions but instead expected others to make sure I was doing well. It was never my fault, but always someone else's.

It was hard to be my friend because I had sky-high expectations and would get mad if someone didn't meet my unspoken wants and desires. I also believed the worst in most situations, walking in fear that the worst possible outcome was usually happening.

You can see how this kind of behavior can make for quite a difficult friendship. At times, my demands and requests were smothering. Being my friend was hard. It depleted others instead of giving them life. All of this was based on fear of being alone. Looking to others to fulfill me, the same issue I had with my wife, was also a major player in this game of dysfunction.

Being Vulnerable and Authentic

Being completely known is one of the most terrifying things a person can choose to do. We all want to put on a smile, wave to the neighbors, and pretend like all is okay. The problem is, rarely is everything okay.

Life is hard. You are an imperfect human. Sometimes life gets difficult.

Sharing how you are truly doing is a hard thing to do, especially if you come from a fatherless home. The fear inside you screams, "If they know you are weak, they will surely leave you. There is no way anyone is going to love you if they know what is actually going on." Plus, as a society, we are not too good at being open and honest about our junk.

The truth is, vulnerably sharing about your hard times is one of the most helpful things you can do. Confessing your need for help and where you went wrong is the first step toward lightening your load (see James 5:16). Being authentic, instead of pretending all is okay is one of the most courageous things you can possibly do. I have found most people, men especially, think being real and showing weakness is something they could never do. But when we are weak, that gives Jesus an opportunity to be strong. Jesus came to heal the sick. The healthy have no need for a savior (see Luke 5:31).

There was a long time when I wouldn't let anyone peek behind the curtain of my soul. No one knew I was hurt, lost, and paralyzed with fear. I pretended like I was the big, strong man who didn't need any help. Emotions were a foreign language to me. No one, not even me, knew who I truly was behind the mask.

Let me tell you. That did not serve me well. It was only when I stopped being fake and admitted that I needed help that the true healthy process could begin. Faith is needed to be vulnerable and authentic. The act of opening yourself up to others whom you trust is saying, "Okay, Lord. I did my part by confessing and being honest. Now it's time for You to do Your part and start the process of healing." It also gives others an opportunity to be the hands and feet of Jesus toward you.

No one is perfect. We all have needs. Might as well be open and honest about it instead of pretending all is well. Trust that the

Lord will see your vulnerability and authenticity, in all your humility and courage, as a sacrifice that is pleasing to Him.

Authority and Receiving Feedback

I remember this event like it was yesterday because the Lord used it to shape the man I am today. It is one of the greatest gifts God has ever given to me.

My mentoring organization was growing rapidly, and it was time for our annual board of directors retreat. My board and I were going to take a few days to review the past year, plan out the upcoming year, and have some fun and fellowship. I was really looking forward to this and saw it as a starting point for an incredible new year.

The five of us were sitting in the living room going over the prior year's accomplishments and shortcomings. I was leading the meeting, and the board members were asking questions for clarification or because they saw something that could make our organization better. The problem is, I would push back and tell them why they were wrong and I was right. I believed I knew more about mentoring than anyone else in the room and shouldn't be questioned.

After a few of these exchanges, my board chairman said, "Every time we bring up something you can improve, you reject it. You aren't listening to us, Zach. If you won't listen to us, then why are we here?"

I didn't understand where he was coming from and thought he was totally off base. I sat there, all eyes on me, and realized I had two options: I could blow up on this guy or I could shut down. Shutting down seemed like the more Christian thing to do.

Head down and not saying a word, I sat there in a pool of failure. That's when the lies of the enemy came:

- "They are all going to leave you."
- "You don't have what it takes to do this job."
- "Everyone is going to find out about this and make fun of you."
- "You're done. You won't have a job, your wife won't love you, and your kids won't respect you."

This story is a good example of how I saw authority. People in charge of me were out to get me and they couldn't be trusted. Why was this? Possibly because the main male authority in my life hurt me and couldn't be trusted. These board members who had authority over me never stood a chance.

From day one, I was on the lookout for how they were going to hurt me. The slightest misstep from them, things like slightly raising their voice or not giving feedback in a gentle enough way, was enough for me to see them as the enemy. I viewed authority not as someone who was there to help me, but as someone who would hurt me.

Authority was hard for me for several reasons, but mostly because I was not used to it. When my dad left, his authority left, too. My mom did the best she could to be an authoritative figure who guided me, but she was busy making ends meet. And a six-foot-eight-inch teenage kid doesn't respond too well to a five-foot-four-inch mom telling him what to do. Until adulthood, I simply did not have to submit to many people. It was a foreign concept to me, as I was used to doing whatever I wanted.

I also didn't receive feedback well because my identity was tied to my performance. If I did something wrong, I was wrong. If my project failed, I was a failure. This stemmed from feeling like I had to earn love. The only time I felt love as a child was when I did something right. Good grades, success in sports, and popularity were what it took to be loved as a child and this carried into adulthood. Success at work meant I was a success. If people questioned how I did things or gave me constructive criticism on how to improve, I would go into "fight or flight" mode, doing whatever I could to show I was right. I wanted to be right so that others would approve of me and ultimately not leave me.

Submission to proper authority and learning from the feedback from others is godly and will set you on a path of success, but I would have none of it. My childhood left me unprepared for these realities.

Being Judgmental

I have come to the conclusion that I am a very judgemental person. Now I know that a lot of people deal with judgment, but I think I am more judgmental than most, and I think it has to do with my childhood. Hear me out...

Being alone most of my life forced me to figure out most things on my own. I'm a lone wolf and most of my successes in life have been because of my efforts. No one else was going to help me, so I did whatever I had to do to be successful. This type of extreme self-reliance, while unhealthy, has caused me to do quite well in this results-oriented world. I have a strong work ethic and a relentless motor, but these actions come from an ugly place. They come from a place of "produce in order to survive." While it may look like I'm striving for excellence, fear truly is my motivator.

Because of that, I look down on anyone who is unsuccessful. In my sinful perspective, they didn't work hard enough, grind long enough, or sacrifice enough to prove their worth. Simply put, they aren't me. They didn't "pull themselves up by their bootstraps," and that causes me to look down on them. Not only that, but I am slow to give grace, have sky-high expectations, and run at a breakneck speed.

Now I know this sounds extremely arrogant and egotistical, and there is probably a lot of that in there. But this ties back to the father wound because it created in me the opinion that you are only as good as what you produce. I only received love when I performed, and I only gave love when others performed. Most of the time, my love is conditional, which is the exact opposite of the love of Christ.

Fear of Failure

I grew up believing I have to perform and be successful in order to be loved. Therefore, I also believed that if I didn't do those things, I would not be loved. My whole life was spent trying to keep it all together and appearing like I was without blemish. The fear of failure, and more importantly losing love, is always in the back of my head. That's what happens when you don't get love from your father for one reason or another.

It only makes sense that I would be apprehensive to admit that I messed up. In my mind, if I confess my mistakes, there is a really good chance you will leave while muttering under your breath, "I knew he'd blow it." You'd take your love with you, too. If I get called out for my mishaps, I'm going to fight tooth and nail to convince you that I was in the right.

This fear also kept me from taking risks. Playing it safe meant that I was a whole lot less likely to fail. It also kept me from apologizing when I fell short or hurt someone.

Even in adulthood, I want to do whatever I can to trick others into loving me. Sometimes that means acting perfect and other times that means covering up my failures. No matter the situation, it's never a good thing to let fear drive your actions.

Extension

Adulthood is not a compartment cut off from the events of childhood. Instead, adulthood is an extension of childhood. For better or worse, childhood is formative. This may leave you enjoying a healthy foundation for life or repairing that foundation for life.

For me, fear was, and still is, a major issue as an adult. Perhaps I couldn't control a lot when I was a child, so I take every opportunity to control what I can now that I'm an adult. I was forced to be self-reliant in my youth and never figured out another way to operate. I find myself having to be in charge often. Here's the kicker: My childhood forced me to grow up before I should have, giving me ample opportunities to be responsible, organized, and disciplined. The choice was to either grow in those areas or be a total failure.

It is those character traits that have led me to be successful in my job. I am responsible and self-motivated. I don't let many things fall through the cracks and I am disciplined to achieve goals when they need to be done. But those exact traits that help me from 9 to 5 hurt me the second I walk in the door at home.

All of these things are a product of growing up feeling alone without the guidance of my father. I thought that once I grew up, I wouldn't have to deal with my father wound anymore and I have found that to be untrue. In fact, adulthood is the perfect time to identify and deal with those wounds. Even now, as you read these words, you have more perspective and experience than ever and are well-suited to face what you may have neglected.

The truth is, unless you deal with the symptoms of your past, they'll just continue wreaking havoc forever. You have to replace the bad habits with good ones, and that takes a ridiculous amount of effort, intentionality, and perseverance. It's a hard process, but one that I believe you can do. Let's talk about what that process looks like next.

Tell Me...

- Do you resonate with any of the issues listed in this chapter? If so, which ones? How have they impacted your life?
- Which areas of your life have been impacted the most by your childhood (for better or worse)? What are a few ways

that affect your relationships, your work, and your family life?

- What are the common fears that you have? How do those play out on a daily basis?

CHAPTER 13

Cleaning Your Lens

I KNOW FOLKS WHO are crazy about dogs. I've seen them treat their dogs like royalty, taking them to fancy dog hotels when they travel and feeding them food that is healthier than the food that I eat. You may be one of them.

Every so often I will go over to someone's house and their dog will run up to greet me. I try to ignore Fido, but some dogs are extremely persistent. The guest will ask what's wrong and I have to tell them the truth.

"I'm not much of a dog person. Don't really care for them."

They are met with amazement. "How can you not like dogs? They're the best!" they say. Well, that may be your experience, but my experience is different.

When I was a child, I got bit by a dog. Nothing major, but the pooch did enough damage to make me leery of dogs. A few months later, I agreed to dogsit for a neighbor who was going out of town for the weekend. Once again, no big deal. Feed the dog. Let it out. Take it on walks. Seems simple enough.

That weekend, the dog threw up all over the house and pooped on the living room floor. I tried to take him on a walk, but he escaped the leash and ran away. I had to chase that dog through the neighborhood for an hour. It was not a pleasant experience.

It was at that moment, running through the neighborhood like a crazy man with doggie teeth marks still fresh on my arm that I decided I'm not a dog guy. They're just not for me.

Now you may have had the perfect dog who has comforted you in times of sadness. You may be that family that has their dog sit in on their family pictures because they were "one of the kids." Your dog may have even saved you from a burning building like Lassie.

If that's the case, it's no surprise that you love dogs. You've had a wonderful experience with them. You may even be tempted to think, "All dogs are like my dog. They are great animals."

But me? I think, "All dogs are like that dog that bit me and threw up everywhere. They are not the best animals."

You might retort, "Not all dogs are bad. You just had a bad experience. I bet if you tried again, you'll find dogs are really pleasant." While that may be true, it may take a while before I build up the courage to give dogs another chance.

Your experience influences how you see certain things. Good experiences usually lead to good perspectives while bad experiences lead to bad perspectives.

For a long time, my experiences led to seeing myself, my dad, and my God wrongly. Those feelings seemed so real to me and they negatively influenced my perspective for a long time and kept me in a place of unforgiveness, shame, and bitterness.

Put simply, the lens through which I saw the world was dirty and needed to be cleaned.

How I Saw My Dad

For a kid who doesn't have a father figure around, "Donuts with Dad" has to be one of the more embarrassing moments of your childhood. While everyone is parading around the school cafeteria showing off their father, you are in the corner by yourself or sitting awkwardly by someone who has come to take the place of your father. While your granddad or youth pastor had good intentions, nothing can make up for the fact that other kids have the one thing you most desperately want: a father.

Events like "Donuts with Dad" pop up from time to time. Whether it's seeing your friend's dad cheering them on at a sporting event or hearing about a father/child campout, events that leave you feeling left out and alone can wreak havoc on your identity. They can make someone feel less than, embarrassed, and ashamed.

Don't even get me started on how Father's Day can crush the soul.

That's why I hated my dad for so long. Sure, he left us and made life for me and my mom more difficult, but he also embarrassed me and made me different from the rest of my friends. He left me alone to be ridiculed by other kids. His absence ensured that every major moment of my life would be incomplete because there would always be something not quite right. I was angry. I was bitter. I was set on making him pay for what he did to me and my mom.

I was able to stuff that anger down in my heart for a long time, decades actually, never giving a second thought as to how that might be negatively impacting me and my heart.

My dad was the selfish jerk who left me. He screwed us over. He was never to be trusted or spoken of again. The experiences I focused on were nothing but negative, therefore my view of him was negative. From my perspective, I had no father. He was dead to me.

How I Saw God

How could God do this to me?

Couldn't He have stopped it?

If God really is good, then why am I experiencing so much hurt?

These are the thoughts that went through my mind. Thoughts that led to feelings of confusion and anger. While I could never articulate these feelings, deep down they were gnawing at me daily.

I could never take these thoughts to God. That would be disrespectful. The Big Guy in the Sky would probably smite me for asking such a thing anyway. Besides, He was probably too busy for me. Like a ruler who did whatever he pleased for no good reason, there was God on His throne just doing whatever He wanted to do whenever He wanted to do it.

If I am being honest, it was probably all my fault to begin with. I didn't pray enough or act good enough. All the things that are happening to me are punishment for my sins. I get it. If I were God, I probably would punish myself too.

How I Saw Self

I hate the word orphan, and I really don't like to use it, but it really is the best word to describe how I felt. Orphanhood was the template for my life. This perspective colored everything I did, said, and thought.

Before prying into this, I want to make it clear: Having parents is not an automatic exemption from an orphan spirit. As you'll see, you could have two parents in the home and still be dominated by orphan-related thinking.

When I think of an orphan, I picture a child living in fear, unsure of who is going to love them or take care of them, and seeing no one to provide for their everyday needs. Their minds are focused on survival, and they do whatever they have to do to get what they need.

While I am thankful I had clothes on my back, a roof over my head, and food to eat, I saw myself as an emotional orphan. Love was not provided for a myriad of reasons, attention had to be fought for, and I was constantly searching for people to give me what my heart needed.

The father wound changes your identity and how you see yourself. It makes you doubt yourself, the goodness of God, and the motives of others. You no longer feel safe or secure, and you are always on the lookout for someone to hurt you. It is hard for you to trust people and to develop intimate relationships that reveal your true self. You feel like you do not have a home where it is safe to love and be loved. You self-protect. You hide. You try to be as self-reliant as possible. And ultimately, you feel you have no other choice. Your survival depends on it.

When Adam and Eve were separated from God, that was the beginning of sin, a heart condition that plagues every human when they enter this world. Because of sin, we are left seeing ourselves as orphans. Like the two children in the story of the prodigal son, we either run away from the father in rebellion like the younger son, or we try to earn the love of the father through performance or religion like the older son. Either way, we as humans choose to go our own way apart from God instead of running toward the presence of the good Father.

I have experienced a lot of shame in my life due to the hand I was dealt. Just the other day I was at a father/son event with my two boys when the leader said, "Okay, fathers, let's go around the circle and talk about the most important thing your father taught you as a kid." I immediately had to confront the shame I felt rising up in my heart.

The spirit of an orphan sees God through a skewed perspective and feels like it must strive harder than anyone else to earn

God's love. The spirit of an orphan can also cause reactions that do not match the experience. For instance, I would overreact or underreact to most things. I'd scream and shout over a little issue or become completely numb when a major event happened in my life. I pulled over and almost fought a guy because he cut me off in traffic but didn't shed a tear when my beloved grandmother passed away.

The spirit of an orphan is easily swayed by circumstances. What is happening around you is what dictates your emotions if you feel like an orphan. For me, I couldn't have a good day if my wife was sad, and I couldn't find joy in the midst of a hard season.

The spirit of an orphan is often overly critical of others, especially those in authority. I would criticize others and make fun of them to build myself up and make myself look better. I had a doctorate in sarcasm. I could dish it out with the best of them but would become angry and defensive if people made fun of me.

The spirit of an orphan doesn't trust anyone. They are lone wolves who often see everybody as the enemy. I consistently believed that people were out to get me and no one would ever want to help someone like me.

The spirit of an orphan caused me to suppress my emotions. The fear of truly being known caused me to close myself off from intimacy with others, replacing it with superficial relationships that focused on making fun of others, sports, or finding girls to hang out with.

The spirit of an orphan has to earn its keep. Perform their way into having a spot at the table. I worked as hard as I could to prove to people that I belonged so that I could earn their conditional love. Receiving anything is difficult, but especially that which I didn't earn. Whether it is help, advice, or financial support, feeling needy just reinforces the lie that I'm not good enough and it's only a matter of time before others leave me because I'm too much of a nuisance.

When you have the spirit of an orphan, sometimes you cannot receive the things that you so desperately desire. Even if someone were to say, "I love you, Zach," the lies of the enemy would convince me that he or she wasn't being honest. Even if a friend said, "Hey man, if you ever want to talk, I'm here for you because I care about you," the enemy's lies persuade me not to open up out of fear I would be seen as weak or the other person would tell my secrets.

Even when I experience the kindness of God the Father, I am always terrified that He's going to pull the rug out from under me while saying, "Just kidding. You're on your own now." It's like an orphan who has been adopted into the perfect family, but can't relax or be happy because they are saying to themselves, "This is good now, but surely this will end. This family can't be this good. I better be thinking about what I'm going to do just in case I get kicked out of here."

The lies of the enemy to the spirit of an orphan are bondage and cause exhaustion. I felt like I had no rest and no place to call home. I felt weary and tired from always having to protect and care for myself. I didn't feel comfortable with others or like I had a true place to be myself. I had to fight to protect what was mine and fight to get what was mine. Fear was a constant companion. I couldn't receive the peace and truth God had for me.

Simply put, I felt alone.

I didn't know what it truly meant to be a son. I never experienced life as a son who was accepted as he was and loved unconditionally.

One of the things you hear said to a child when their parents split up is, "It's not your fault." While, in most cases, the separation has little to do with the actions of a child, the enemy can use the separation as an invitation to lay a foundation of lies. The lies sound a little bit like this:

- "If you were a better kid, your dad would have stuck around."
- "Your father doesn't love you. If he did, he wouldn't have left."
- "You're not worth it. If you were, your dad would still be here."

When you speak these lies out loud, they seem absurd. Any logical adult knows these statements are not true. But for children who have just had their lives turned upside down, these thoughts do not sound crazy. In fact, they start to make a lot of sense.

If I had a summary statement about my perspective during that time, it might sound a little something like this:

- I am forgotten by God.
- I am scared and hiding.
- God messed up when He made me.
- I do just enough to get by, and I think only about myself.
- I am a chameleon, only acting with integrity and respect if it'll benefit me.
- I don't feel loved. I don't forgive because they'll just hurt me again.
- I am a disappointment to my Heavenly Father.
- I try to be good to impress Jesus and earn His love.
- The Holy Spirit wants nothing to do with a guy like me.

I know these sound crazy, but that is legitimately how I viewed myself until the Lord changed my perspective. These lies don't stay in childhood, either. They can permeate throughout decades. I know men in their forties and fifties whose identities are still influenced by events that happened when they were a child. Honestly speaking, I still deal with a lot of these lies, and I'm a grown man.

How you see determines who you will be. What you believe about God determines what you receive from God. If you believe He is stingy, cold, and distant, you will not position yourself to receive His lovingkindness.

Similarly, if you believe that you are not worth pouring into, you will remove your capacity to receive any good thing.

As humans, we are suckers for first impressions. The early impressions that a person or place makes on us can be very difficult to upend. Research shows that we form an impression of someone within the first seven seconds of meeting them.[4] Here's the crazy thing. Harvard did a study that showed that it takes eight subsequent encounters with someone in order to reverse the initial impression we had of them.[5]

If we do this on a day-to-day basis with people we meet, how much more are children susceptible to early impressions? Cleaning your lenses, so to speak, and reversing these mental templates is hard work but worthy work. And oftentimes, I have to clean my lens multiple times a day.

Adopt God's vision of others, yourself, and Him. This new perspective might be jarring at first. That's okay. You've had bad vision for a long time, and now you're seeing the world crisp and clear with a new prescription.

Your actions follow your perspective. Jesus said, "The eye is the lamp of the body; so if your eye is clear [spiritually perceptive], your whole body will be full of light [benefiting from God's precepts]" (Matthew 6:22-23 AMP).

Healing the father wound is as much about clearing your vision as it is removing your pain.

Tell Me...

- Can you point to a time in your life when you experienced a radical shift in perspective on something? What were the short and long-term consequences of this?
- We've talked a lot about how you see your father, yourself, and God. Did this chapter reveal anything new about your perspective? Do you feel your view of your dad, yourself, and God are all in top shape? Why or why not?

- Do any of the symptoms of the orphan spirit show up in your life? If so, when was a time that you experienced feeling like an orphan?

CHAPTER 14

The Three-Legged Stool

THE APOSTLE PAUL was no theological lightweight. The guy knew his stuff. Not only was he a massive contributor to the New Testament, but he was an Old Testament scholar who was fluent in Greek, Hebrew, and possibly even Latin. Despite his knowledge of the depths and complexities of the Scriptures, we can reasonably boil down his message to three simple words; faith, hope, and love.

These are the three legs of the stool that keep the whole thing balanced and standing. If you remove one, the stool falls. All three are necessary to be upheld and on track. Paul instructed the Corinthians, saying, "And now abide faith, hope, love, these three; but the greatest of these is love" (1 Corinthians 13:13-14 NKJV). He continued the theme in his letter to the Thessalonians, "...remembering without ceasing your work of *faith*, labor of *love*, and patience of *hope* in our Lord Jesus Christ in the sight of our God and Father" (1 Thessalonians 1:3 NKJV, emphasis added).

In the process of dealing with my relationship with my father, I felt like I had the exact opposite of these verses. My works and actions were produced by fear, not faith. My labor and the things that I did were prompted by a feeling of having to earn love. I did not understand unconditional love. I pressed on in endurance, not because I had hope in Jesus, but because the root behind my hope was to create my own sense of security. I had to earn my spot at the table or else God would give my spot to someone else.

In conversations with people who have an absent father, they share about their past and how much it has impacted them today, but more times than not they say something like this, "Because I grew up without my father around, it has made me want to be the best parent I can be." Their pain has fueled their passion. The curse has turned into a blessing.

I have found that people who grew up without a father figure in the home typically either run away from their parental responsibilities, just like their father did, or they do the opposite and take their job as a father extremely seriously. If you are reading this book, I am assuming you fall into the second camp.

I don't know if it is because of my wiring or because of my past experiences, but I've wanted to be a father for as long as I can remember. Concerning basically anything negative attributed to growing up without a father, I say in my head, "I may have experienced that, but my kids for sure won't." I want to give them the childhood that I never had and keep them from the childhood that I had.

Where I had little oversight, I made sure my kids had the highest quality education and a love for reading. I monitor what they watch and what they eat, and I make sure they see that my wife and I enjoy being with each other. All of these intentional acts are motivated by the knowledge of what I never had.

While on the outside this seems like a noble and intentional way of living, I have come to question the fuel behind my actions. I began to evaluate my motives when my responses to certain disappointments were out of whack.

For instance, how do I handle myself when my kids complain during vacation? What's my response when they don't want to have deep, philosophical conversations at the dinner table? What is my reaction when my kids watch too much TV or complain when we make them read a book?

For me, the answer has been: *not good*. From time to time, I overreact. I scream. I shout. I make them feel terrible about themselves.

Why do I do that? Why do I get so angry when they don't do exactly what I say and value the things that I know will lead to their best life? I'm sure that's a loaded question, but I have come to the conclusion that the root of why I behave the way that I do comes down to one word: fear.

Simply put, I am absolutely terrified that my kids are going to have the childhood that I had. I am fearful that I am going to be a bad parent. I am scared that the past is going to repeat itself and my hopes for producing a generational blessing will actually be a continuation of my generational curse. My orphan mindset says, "God will fail you. He won't provide. You are on your own."

As I follow my fears to assess where they are coming from, I realize that I had been scared long before I was married. As a single man, the fear of being alone for the rest of my life nearly drove me insane. In retrospect, it turns out that I was afraid almost constantly, even if I looked secure and confident on the outside. I was fearful people wouldn't like me and nervous that people would leave. I was scared to be left out and scared other people wouldn't invite me to their parties. I was afraid I wouldn't perform well in school or in sports and afraid to take risks or try new things.

The main fear that I had in general was that I would mess everything up. That I am going to lose it all. Naturally, a generic lie like this will find its way into the most consequential areas of life: marriage and family.

I was genuinely scared that I would be a bad husband and a bad father, thus ruining the lives of my wife and children. It does not take a ton of imagination to see how it's possible to ruin a family. If I'm being honest with you, most of them don't seem too far-fetched.

What if I lost my job and couldn't provide financially for my household? How about drinking too much one night and making a terrible mistake? Perhaps my wife just gets tired of me and my antics and decides to up and leave.

My grandparents had a terrible marriage, my own parents couldn't make it work, and the logical flow meant I should be doomed for a bad marriage. With no one to turn to and very little support, it seemed like the odds of having a good marriage were stacked against me. Outside the home, most of my friends' parents were divorced or had bad marriages as well. If someone was going to screw this up, I was a great candidate.

Those are the paralyzing fears that went through my head on a pretty consistent basis. The rotten fruit was low self-confidence, hopelessness, anxiety, and depressive thought patterns.

In truth, people have a hard time doing something they have never done before. Even fewer people like doing things that scare them. Safe to say that doing something scary that you have never done before is a terrifying experience. That was me when signing up to be a husband. When my father left, the example to follow went with him.

What do I do when my wife needs words of affirmation? What about helping with chores around the house or working together to discipline our children? What about intimacy, supporting my wife during pregnancy, or dealing with marital conflict in a healthy way?

Besides six weeks of premarital counseling, all of those topics were new to me as I entered marriage. It's like someone tossed me a tennis racket for the first time and said, "By the way, you have a really long match tomorrow. It's actually going to last the rest of your life. Also, it's probably going to be the most important thing you do in your life. Good luck."

My mindset going into our wedding day was not that I was suited to be a rockstar husband. Instead, I felt like I would be a subpar spouse. I was starting from hopelessness.

If marriage sounds hard, which it is, just wait until you toss a few little kiddos in the mix. As if selflessly serving my wife wasn't enough, now I have to do it while changing diapers, losing sleep, and trying to communicate with my wife over the sound of a crying baby.

Also, you have to provide financially and emotionally for every member of your household.

I stood in the shadows of this tall order, thoroughly intimidated.

Living with the pressure to hold everything together was a big burden to carry, especially with little to no training. The stakes were high, and I obsessed over worst-case scenarios.

For instance, one day, my son came home from school with a note from his teacher explaining the upcoming end-of-the-year history project. This was the biggest project in his second-grade class and would make up 25% of the final grade. It was a doozy of an assignment, but we had a month to prepare for it. The teacher wanted the students to do three things: create an art project describing the topic, dress up in a costume that represents that topic, and memorize a 2-minute speech describing their chosen subject.

It was a lot, but I was excited to help my son ace it. I thought to myself, "We have a month to prepare, we'll get to it later."

Big mistake.

A few weeks later, my eight-year-old son came home from school with some shocking news.

"Dad. My history project is due tomorrow."

"What?"

"What are we going to do?"

"Uhhhhh..."

Panic ensues. To make matters worse, my wife was out of town and it was my job to hold down the fort and take care of all three of our kids. I went into drill sergeant mode and started ordering my son around like this was boot camp.

"Go get the note cards. Grab the markers. Find the poster board. Get your books out. Let's do this."

I continued on like that for hours. We made the poster. We wrote the notecards so that he could practice memorizing all of his lines. We found a costume for him to wear.

As he was practicing his speech, I began to correct him relentlessly.

"Speak louder."

"Keep your head up."

"You're mispronouncing that word."

After about ten minutes of that, my son burst into tears. Immediately, I realized what I had done: I let my fear get the best of me.

I went into drill sergeant mode, not because I really cared a ton about his project, but because I didn't want him to fail. In my head, the spiral went something like this:

"If he fails this project then he will get a bad grade. If he gets bad grades, he won't go to college and get a good job. Even worse, if he fails this project, he will make a fool out of himself on stage and everyone will laugh at him. Then he won't have any friends. All of this is my fault. My son won't be able to get a good job, and he won't have any friends because I dropped the ball on this project. I knew it. I'm a bad dad, and my son is going to suffer for it."

As I look back now, I ask myself, "What's the worst that could have happened?" This is a great question to ask yourself when you find yourself in a fear cycle. That single question is like a shock treatment to get you back into reality.

Worst case scenario: My kid failed a second-grade history project and got embarrassed in front of his friends and wonderful teacher. His life wouldn't have been over. He would be okay. In fact, it probably wouldn't even be that big of a deal to him in the grand scheme of things. However, fear can motivate some intense responses.

Hero or Hermit

Fear, taken to its end, usually plays out in one of two ways. You will either play the hero or hide as a hermit.

The hero is the one who looks like he or she has it all together and has no weaknesses to speak of. When I play the hero, I try to be the all-star on the sports team or the wild man at the party. I volunteer for everything, and I don't show any weakness whatsoever. I never ask for help, and I'll do whatever you tell me to do.

The hermit is the one who knows they don't have it together, so they don't even bother to try. They do nothing because they have already presumed failure as the outcome. Try something new? No way. I know I can't do it. Attempt a romantic relationship? Why would someone want to be with me? They have come to the conclusion that life is just so much easier if you just hide.

If you find yourself not feeling loved, the easy thing to do is to just check out completely and live a risk-free life of isolation and despair. The problem is, you actually risk everything.

Others take the opposite approach and chase the non-solution of *earning* love through performance. This falls apart sooner or later because genuine love is not grounded in what people do but in *who people are.*

In my insecurity, I oscillate between hero and hermit often. One moment I am pretending to be Superman and the next I am in my room isolated drowning in lies. Both the Hero and the Hermit are built upon shaky foundations. The Hero hears, "Just hold it all together. If they find out you are a fake, you're done," while the Hermit believes, "It's just best if you don't do anything. We all know how this is going to end."

The hero is often wrapped up in self-promotion, and the hermit is caught up in self-deprecation, but God calls us to healthy self-worth. Rest assured, God does not want you to be torn between hero and hermit, but instead to find yourself as a humble child of His.

Perhaps your father gave you a bad stool to sit on. Your life has been anything but balanced and stability is a pipe dream. That was certainly the case for me. The enemy would like to maintain a twisted three-legged stool in your life made of fear, hopelessness, and self-hatred. God, though, is interested in flipping the script and replacing fear with faith, hopelessness with hope, and self-hatred with love.

Tell Me...

- Seeing myself as an orphan is something that rears its ugly head often and causes me to walk in insecurity. What are some ways that you may find yourself walking out in insecurity?
- Do you relate more to the hero or the hermit? Tell me why.
- How has your relationship with your father impacted your view on faith, hope, and love?

CHAPTER 15

Experience Required

EXPERIENCE TRUMPS KNOWLEDGE. You can debate doctrine all day long, but you cannot move a man who has had an encounter.

Growing up in the church, I had knowledge but lacked experience. The truth is, I knew a lot of men who would preach about being kind and helping the poor, but yelled at me when I misbehaved and didn't help my mom and me when we were struggling. This didn't make sense to me. Why would I want to follow Jesus if I didn't respect His followers?

To me, church was all about rules and looking good. It was all discipline and correction. It wasn't fun, and I left feeling ashamed every Sunday. Why would anyone want to be a part of that?

I knew a lot *about* God the Father, but I didn't personally know God the Father. It was similar to being able to tell all the facts about your favorite athlete or movie star, but you've never actually met them. I could tell you most of the things the Bible said about God, but I had never experienced His kindness and mercy for myself. I knew in my mind that God was good, but that wasn't what I experienced.

In my late twenties, I started on a journey to find out if I wanted to follow Jesus Christ and call Him the Lord of my life. I was on the fence, but then I met Larry.

I was introduced to Larry through a discipleship program. Everyone in the program seemed to hold Larry in high regard. Turns out, he had been in the ministry for over 35 years, and he had a real gift of encouragement.

After a time of prayer during this program, Larry approached me and asked if he could encourage me with a prophetic word. I agreed and he said:

> "I just want to encourage you. When you were praying, I felt that God was unsticking your button. You've been trying to get your button unstuck for a long time and the reason it is stuck is because of your upbringing. This is your year of reset and retooling. I want to encourage you as a father that God's will for your life is so broad that you can fall down and not miss it. Like David, you are a good man and you delight in the way of God. Some of the things you deal with go back a few generations in your family line. God is working on that. There will be a day in your life when people will say that you were an incredible father. What you didn't receive from a father you will become one hundred-fold. You will be known as a shepherd, father, and an innovator in your old age. Somewhere in your early teen years, something traumatic happened and it put a weight on you. The Lord is removing that weight. You were in jail, but God has set you free."

I knew that God sent this man to give me hope and to let me know that He was real and was for me and not against me. When Larry shared the Lord's words with me, I could feel the presence of God during that experience. I walked into that room one way and left a totally different person. Experiencing the love of God will do that to you.

Equipped with a new perspective, I started attending churches that were unlike any other I had experienced. It seemed like everyone had tattoos and was dressed in super-expressive ways. Everyone I met was either an entrepreneur, artist, or hairdresser. They valued the arts, creativity, and freedom. While I loved these new churches and was growing in my faith, I soon realized these have their shortcomings as well. Sometimes they valued feelings over Scripture, which left me uneasy. It took me a long time to realize that churches run by humans will never be perfect.

One day, I was complaining about the denomination I was brought up in to a friend and boasting about my new wonderful church. My friend was patient as he listened to me badmouth the former church. Finally, after I was done ranting, he said, "Zach, there is no such thing as a perfect church. Do you know why? Because church is full of imperfect people. I want you to read John 4:23-24. I also want you to know that every church does some things well and could use help in other areas. I bet you wouldn't be here today if it wasn't for the church you grew up in. They probably made more of an impact on you than you think. The church is the bride of Jesus. He loves it in all its imperfections, just like He does with you."

I went home and opened John 4:23-24 that next morning: "But the hour is coming, and is now here, when the true worshipers will worship the Father in spirit and truth, for the Father is seeking such people to worship him. God is spirit, and those who worship him must worship in spirit and truth."

That's when it hit me. True worshippers will worship in spirit and truth. It's not an either/or type thing, but a both/and.

God created all people to be an expression of Him—the type A accountant who is highly logical is just as much a part of God as the free-spirit creative who lives for experiences. I can learn from both. Everybody can be my teacher if I give them the chance. I shouldn't talk badly about His people or church because they were all made to represent the Lord. Instead, I should champion both.

True worshipers will worship in spirit. This means I can fully worship the Lord with my hands held up high. I will experience the power of the Holy Spirit and will embrace the gifts of God. I can be open to the things I don't understand and give grace when things don't go as I'd like. I will grow in my creativity and thank God who wired me as an entrepreneur.

True worshippers also worship in truth. This means I can become a student of the Word. I will grow in the daily disciplines and study the Bible to gain more knowledge.

That day I realized that God has wired all of us to enjoy Him personally. I do believe that we are all naturally bent toward a particular way of worshiping Him, and it is our responsibility to discover what that is.

Once I arrived at this revelation, I made it my mission to take the truth that I knew about God and put it into experience. I knew God was a good Father. I understood that He was a God of compassion and mercy. But in the past, I didn't know what it felt like to receive His compassion and mercy.

As a human being, you tend to believe experiences over truth. I can tell you all day long that God is a good Father. There's even a song about it. I can show you the verses on His love and tell you about all the godly people who say great things about "their daddy in Heaven." However, if you've experienced hurt, pain, and a broken family, you might not believe me or care what the Bible says.

I had a lot of experience with people telling me that God the

Father was a God of comfort, but I didn't know what actual comfort felt like. I knew in my head that God was love, but my heart yearned to be unconditionally loved by someone.

It was time for me to have some hard conversations with God. I wanted to *experience* the love of God the Father. I wanted the things I knew about Him to actually happen in my life. I desired to not just talk about God and what He is like; I wanted to meet Him face-to-face. I had to know what an intimate, personal relationship with my Father was like.

It reminds me of the story of Zaccheus in Luke 19. Zaccheus was looking for God when the person of Jesus Christ approached him. Jesus didn't ask for his to-do list or his list of achievements. He pursued him because he loved him, in all his junk. Zacchaeus did nothing to earn the presence of Jesus.

"Zacchaeus, come down immediately. I must stay at your house today." That day, Zaccheus experienced God in a new way. His encounter with Jesus changed his heart, which changed his actions. It was an inside shift that created an outside shift, all because he experienced the person of Jesus. I wanted that. I wanted Jesus to come to me just like he did Zaccheus. I wanted an encounter to change my heart.

My relationship with God changed in profound ways as I began to experience Him as a good Father. I began to see Him as the father in the story of the prodigal son in Luke:

> "But while he was still a long way off, his father saw him and was filled with compassion for him; he ran to his son, threw his arms around him and kissed him. The son said to him, 'Father, I have sinned against Heaven and against you. I am no longer worthy to be called your son.' But the father said to his servants, 'Quick! Bring the best robe and put it on him. Put a ring on his finger and sandals on his feet. Bring the fattened calf and kill it. Let's have a feast and celebrate. For this son of mine was dead and is alive again; he was lost and is found.' So they began to celebrate." (Luke 10:20-22)

Allow me to dial in on five distinct phrases from this text that took the scripture from being educational to being experiential for me.

First, the parable goes, "But while he was a long way off...." It's clear that God is on the lookout for you. He wants to be with you so badly that He is constantly looking to see when you will come around. For me, when I realized this, I knew it was something I had never felt from a father before.

"His father saw him...." I am visible to God. He sees me. In the middle of everything He has going on, He takes time out for me. He knows what I'm going through. He sees my issues and the things on my mind. He sees me and cares for me because I am important to Him.

"He ran to his son, threw his arms around him, and kissed him" showed me that my Father is willing to do anything to show me how much He loves me. He'll run through town if that's what it takes to be with me. He'll throw His arms around me and give me a big hug no matter what condition I find myself in. He'll kiss a grown man and doesn't care who is watching. He is willing to do whatever it takes to show His heart for me, His son.

"Bring the best robe and put it on him. Put a ring on his finger" expressed to me that I was worth things of great value because I am of great value. "Only the best for my son" is the feeling that I get when I think of how my Father in Heaven wants to lavish me with extravagant gifts.

"Let's have a feast and celebrate" communicates to me that I am worth celebrating. Not only does my Father want to be with me, but He wants to throw a party to celebrate who I am. He is proud of me. He wants to show me off. He has invited all of His friends over to say, "Look at my son. Isn't he something? Come and sit with me as I learn all that is going on with him over a delicious dinner."

My relationship with God the Father changed when my understanding of how God saw me changed. I've always known that God loves me, but now I have experienced His love. And experience trumps knowledge every time. Instead of just doing my typical, "Yeah, yeah, He values me. He cares for me. I get that," I actually took the time to imagine and receive God valuing me and caring for me. And this is what I pray you will do as well.

Tell Me...

- How can you reconcile the unfortunate events in your life with God being a good Father?
- Do you relate to the story of the prodigal son, either as the younger or older brother? Are there insights in the story that apply to your own? How does the father in that story paint a picture of God the Father, and how does that differ from your experience?

CHAPTER 16

Sonship

I CAN REMEMBER HOW I felt the day that I became a father. To say that day was special for me doesn't begin to describe the magnitude of the event. Hands down, it was one of the greatest moments in my life.

To hold my son for the first time was a surreal encounter. As I sat in the chair with him in my arms, I couldn't help but stare into his dark brown eyes. For what seemed like an hour, we just looked at each other. And at that moment, my heart developed a love I'd never experienced before. I can't put it into words, but I just knew this love was different from the love I had for my wife or my friends.

I cannot even begin to explain how much I love my kids. If you're a parent, you know the feeling. From the moment they came into this world, they had my heart. I would do anything for my children. I take very seriously the call to protect, guide, and do whatever I have to do to ensure they are set up for success. I love being with them. They don't have to earn the love of their father. I love them because they are mine, and nothing can take away that love.

Here's the crazy thing: God loves you *so much* more than that. God's love makes earthly paternal and maternal love look amateur. When God looks upon you, He sees His child with whom He is well pleased. His face lights up. You don't have to earn or perform to get God to love you. He loves you because you are His child. His love flows straight from the goodness and kindness of God. All our Heavenly Father wants is to be with His children. And as His sons and daughters, we can be secure knowing we are covered by their Father. That's *sonship*, and it's probably a little different than what you've experienced.

The Beginning of Sonship

What does it mean to enter into sonship? You can find the beginning of sonship in the Garden and Eden. When God created the Earth, there was no sin and everything was perfect. God created man and woman in His image—a true work of art. God took His time on man and woman. Once created, He blessed them and took care of them. He set them up for success and gave them everything they needed to thrive. He called them to be fruitful, to multiply, and to create an abundance of the things that brought them joy.

Adam and Eve were living a life of dependency and intimacy with their Father. Whatever they needed, physically and emotionally, the Father was there to take care of them. They were always in His presence. God was their Father, and they were His children— His pride and joy, His everything.

There was no lack. Instead, there was an invitation to fill the Earth with good things and oversee it. They were in charge, and the Lord trusted them to do a great job. God gave them food through plants and animals to manage. Beauty was everywhere. It was perfect. Our minds cannot even comprehend what the Garden of Eden was like. When He was finished, God looked around and was satisfied. His masterpiece wasn't just good, it was *very* good.

Everything that I just described—that's sonship.

Then sin messed everything up.

Because of the sin of man, a wall was built between man and God. There was a separation because God cannot have anything to do with sin. It goes against His perfect nature. But God had a plan.

God the Father sent God the Son, Jesus, down to Earth to redeem what was broken and to reconcile His children. The death of Jesus dismantled the wall that sin built between God the Father and His children.

I used to think God was this old man sitting on His chair waiting for me to mess up so that He could scold me. I thought He loved me only when I did right and focused only on my mess-ups. Never in a thousand years did I believe that He was a compassionate Father who was willing to move Heaven and Earth to show His love to me.

Your identity is no longer that of an orphan. Your identity is now that of a son or daughter, a child of God.

You may have spent the first part of your life thinking a certain way and perceiving life through one set of lenses. Now everything has changed. You are now free to stop thinking like an orphan and start thinking like a son or daughter of the King.

I was spending time with my son the other day, and he was telling me about a problem he had at school. He didn't know how to do a problem in math class, and a kid was poking fun at him. I sat my son down, and I asked him if he was worried about school or the issues he was having. He turned to me and said, "No, I'm not worried at all, Dad. I know you'll take care of me and help me if I have any problems."

One day, my son will realize that I, his earthly father, will fail him in one way or another. After all, I'm not perfect. But my son also has a Father on his side who *is* perfect. A Father who will never fail him or forsake him, a Father he can count on no matter what.

As a son of God, I am free to believe that my Father is who He says He is. The confidence my son has in me erodes worry and fear, so it should be the same as how I view my Father in Heaven.

As a son of God, I can let Him be in control. I can depend on Him instead of myself. When we let go of control of our life, and ask God to lead, we'll never know where the Lord may take us, but we *can* know it'll be good. As a son of the Most High, it is no longer up to you to control things, but instead, you have faith that the Lord will take care of you and the Holy Spirit will guide you. You can let go and rest, knowing that you are in the Lord's good hands.

Through abiding as a son and daughter of the Lord, you produce the fruit of the Holy Spirit. Love replaces hate and joy dismantles negativity. You are patient, never forcing your own way in your own timing out of fear. You are kind instead of sarcastic and gentle when you were once angry. Your life is marked by peace, and you walk in goodness and self-control. You live not with a spirit of fear, but with a spirit of power because the love of God has been poured into your heart, filling you up so that you can spread that love to others.

The Promises of Sonship

In the eyes of a child, there is nothing stronger than the promise of a father. When a godly dad promises his son to do something, consider it done. Our Heavenly Father is the same way. His promises are better than that of a good father; His promises will never fail you.

In fact, as sons and daughters of God, His promises are not just promises, but they are part of the inheritance He is handing down to us. It's more than a guarantee or a wish list. It is His legal will.

My five-year-old son loves nothing more than a good bike ride around the neighborhood. Having just learned how to ride a bike this past summer, he's extremely proud of the fact that he can ride his bike without training wheels. My wife and I love to watch him go. The only rule we have is he has to ride with Dad because our street can get pretty busy.

One day, I came home from work, and my son met me in my driveway, asking if we could go ride bikes. It was one of those days where the only thing I wanted to do was change into my sweatpants and turn on the TV. I gave my son the ole, "We'll do it later," and hoped he would forget about it.

My son, the persistent one, waited about three minutes before asking me again if we could go ride. In a daze, I said, "After dinner, son."

"Do you promise?" he said.

"Yeah, sure," I answered and didn't think about it again.

Well, my son did think about it again. As soon as dinner was over, he said, "Dad, let's go ride bikes."

"It's too dark outside," I told him.

He looked at me with tears in his eyes. "But Dad, you promised."

Three minutes later we were riding around the neighborhood in the pitch black.

The last thing I was going to do was build an idea in my son that my word was no good. After all, I'm working to model God whose word we can take to the bank all day, every day. He simply cannot be anything other than faithful. It's who He is.

Littered throughout Scripture we see a rich banquet of promises, aimed directly at the sons and daughters of God. The sentiments are clear: God is good to all. His compassion is for all. His love endures forever, and His faithfulness continues to all generations. He gives good and perfect gifts to His children. He never changes. His promises are trustworthy, and He has promised good things to you. Blessed is the one who takes refuge in the Lord. He cares for those who trust in Him alone. He withholds nothing from those whose walk is blameless. He gives strength to the weary and power to the weak. Those who hope in the Lord will renew their strength. They will not grow weary. When you pass through the waters, He will be with you. When you walk through the fire, you will not be burned.

For the Lord has plans for you to prosper. He gives you hope and a future. He will not harm you. Nor will He ever leave you or abandon you. He goes before you and will be with you always. Do not be discouraged. Do not be afraid. Even though you may walk through the darkest valley, the Lord will be with you. There is no reason to be afraid, as He will comfort you. When in need, ask God, who will replace your anxiety with peace. God knows what you need and will provide. The Lord will make your path straight. He is a good Father who gives good gifts to those who ask. You will be successful in every good work because God will bless you with all that you need. Those who seek the Lord lack no good thing. For God did not spare His own Son. How will He not also graciously give us all things? If you are weary and burdened, go to the Lord. He will give you rest. He is gentle and humble in all His ways. Jesus is the way, the truth, and the life.

Whoever follows Him will never walk in darkness. The Holy Spirit will help you. He will teach you all things and remind you when you forget. The Lord will bind up the broken-hearted and release the prisoners from darkness. He has come to give life and life to the fullest. He will listen to you and will respond to your prayers. He is near to all who call on Him. He is with you always, even to the end of the age. If you lack wisdom, all you have to do is ask Him for it and He will freely give it to you. If you ask for something in prayer and believe that you will receive it, it will be yours.

When you take delight in the Lord, He will give you the desires of your heart. Whatever you ask in His name, He will do it. Ask and it will be given. Seek and you will find. Knock and the door will be opened to you. For God so loved the world that He gave His one and only Son. And if the Son sets you free, you are free indeed. If we confess our sins, He is faithful to forgive us and purify us. The Lord is patient toward you, not wishing that any should perish, but that all should reach repentance. God is a Father to the fatherless.

I could chew on the promises of God for the rest of my life and still not understand how He is this good. This is our Father. Does it sound too good to be true? It does. But that's how good our Father is.

Abiding in Sonship

Instead of focusing on bearing fruit or trying to wrestle these promises into your life, the role of a son or daughter is to simply abide and be connected to the Father—to be with Him, fully dependent on receiving all that you need from Him. This can be hard because I have very little experience with being the son of a good father. The experience I do have is not positive. I do not know how to rest in the arms of a father. It's a foreign concept to me.

How do we know if we are abiding in God? Look at the fruit. "Whoever says he abides in him ought to walk in the same way which he walked" (1 John 2:6). And "Whoever keeps his commandments abides in God and God in him" (1 John 3:24).

Does a branch have to strive to be a part of the tree? No. It just is. We can be the same way with God. Just like a tree and a branch, being connected is simply a way of life. God says that if you abide in Him, you will bear much fruit. Your heart will desire the things of God instead of the things of this earth.

Identity in Sonship

When someone first pointed out my inability to receive compliments, I played it off as trying to be humble. But really, it was because I didn't believe I was worthy to be praised. My self-esteem was too low, and I didn't have an accurate view of myself. I couldn't see myself as the Lord saw me. I was used to seeing myself through the eyes of this world instead of through the eyes of a father.

Now, as His son, I can be grateful for all that the Lord has done through me. I can receive praise and tell how good God has been to me. I can receive love because I see myself as loved by God. I can receive praise because I believe the Lord made me *on* purpose *for* a purpose. When I look in the mirror, I don't see all the things I have done wrong. Instead, I see a son of God who is being used to advance the kingdom.

A son and daughter can freely receive from their father without guilt or shame. They know who they are and whose they are. Their identity is secure. As a son or daughter of God, you may even find yourself believing the following:

- Confidence in the Lord's ability to take care of me and to provide for my every need is available to me. You can feel secure in who you are and who God created you to be. You don't need to pretend anymore because who you are is enough. You were made on purpose and for a purpose.
- Your relationship with your father and your childhood does not have to bring you as much pain and shame as it once did. You can talk about your father without negative emotions rising. If you do find yourself holding on to unforgiveness or bitterness, you can more quickly give it to the Lord and deal with it.
- You can walk in a culture of honor and do everything that you can to stay positive. You may even find yourself celebrating other people's successes and putting them in a position to succeed. You now realize there is enough blessing and favor to go around and that God has a different mission for each of His sons and daughters.
- You no longer are afraid to be in touch with your emotions. In fact, you are now grateful that you can recognize and deal with your emotions in such a way that keeps you

healthy and ensures that your heart is right with God. Being authentic and vulnerable with people helps keep you humble, and facing your emotions helps you process potential hurts and pains.

- Submission to authority has now become a staple in your life. You know the security and covering authority brings and you welcome their feedback and observations.
- You believe the best in people, knowing that they are doing their best and trying their hardest. You expect good things to happen and are quick to celebrate others.
- You can rest knowing that you are enough for the Lord. His approval is all that you need. You now walk in security, knowing that you are exactly where the Lord wants you to be.
- You are quick to forgive others because Jesus Christ has forgiven you. You do not hold grudges and reject bitterness.
- Your motive has changed from trying to please others to trying to please God. You are focused on making Him happy, knowing that if you live to please God and do what He wants you to do, it is there that you will be most satisfied with life. Of course, you still sin and fall short of perfection, but that is not who you are. You are a lot more focused on the grace and kindness of God the Father than on your performance or behavior.
- You do not allow circumstances to control your emotions. You have the confidence needed to face difficult situations, and you handle yourself with maturity and wisdom.
- You recognize disciplines like praying, reading your Bible, and going to church are all things that help you grow closer to the Lord. They are your way of being with Him, not some requirement to receive His love.

When the Lord showed Himself as my perfect Father, I entered into sonship. Over time, I felt like I had worth because the Creator of the universe wanted to be with me. One thing that helped me tremendously in seeing myself as God saw me was repeating my vision statement over myself every morning in the mirror.

If you don't have one, I would encourage you to do so. Feel free to use or modify mine as needed in your own life:

I am a man of God.

I am strong, fearless, and courageous.
I am a man after God's own heart.
I walk in wisdom and power.
I have favor with God and man.

I live life to the fullest.
I was created on purpose, for a purpose.
I act with responsibility, humility, integrity, leadership, and respect.
I am loved and will love others with the love of Jesus.
I will forgive because I am forgiven.

I surround myself with godly friends.
I honor women with my words and actions.
I will be a godly husband, father, and leader.

I am loved by my Heavenly Father.
I am saved by grace through faith in Jesus.
I am empowered by the Holy Spirit.

I am a man of God.

Amen.

At first, those words made me feel awkward and insecure. But over time, I came to truly see myself as the Lord saw me. And the shift in identity changed my life.

Experiencing God as a Father and, as a result, walking in sonship, was a watershed event for me. Most importantly, it shifted how I thought. I went from believing the worst about people and situations to believing the best. I no longer assumed the worst because I knew God, my good Father, was in charge of it all. Knowing that my Heavenly Father is for me, not against me, shattered my foundation of lies and replaced it with truth and faith.

Through my newfound identity, the Lord transformed my mind. I could now do things that I could never do before—like believe the best when someone gave me hard feedback or forgive someone when they wronged me. Whenever I spent time with the Lord, I was filled with His presence and my mind was renewed with His purposes.

The highest compliment imaginable has already been given. It's not that God calls you a servant, a slave, or a colleague. Instead, He has extended the unthinkably high title of "son" to you. Embrace your identity, and watch your world shift. Father wounds cannot cling to the hearts of those who know they are true sons of the Most High.

Tell Me...

- Which bullet point in the "identity in sonship" resonates with you the most? Why do you think it hits home?
- How does the concept of "adoption" register with you? God has adopted us into His family, and He has chosen us despite all of our flaws and shortcomings. What does this say about His heart for you?
- Which promises in the scriptures listed above stick out to you the most? Why do you feel a connection to those verses in particular?

CHAPTER 17

The Packing List

I N MY JOURNEY of identifying, processing, and healing the pain in my relationship with my father, I kept coming across the same ethereal advice that made it seem so easy to get to my destination of freedom. People would say, "Just forgive your dad," "Get over your anger," and, "It's time to move on past your pain."

I can remember one time in particular early on in my journey when I was at a men's retreat with about three dozen men of all ages. In our small groups, we started talking about the father-heart of God and how we see God as Father. Of course, this gave me a silver platter to discuss my journey, how my childhood has impacted me, and my view of God the Father.

After I shared, awkwardness filled the air. No one knew what to say. Finally, an older man who was a successful businessman and highly regarded in his church stood up and grabbed me by the shoulders. He looked me in the eyes and said intensely, "It's time to get over that. Just stop. I don't want to hear any more about your father."

I stood there motionless, but one thought immediately came to mind:

"I want to get over it, but I don't know how."

No restoration story is the same. You can, however, find some common themes in most redemptive father-wound stories. My aim in this section is to give you a loose blueprint for action steps to consider as you go about healing the father wound. I don't have all the answers, and I know every journey will be different, but I hope this at least gives you some support as you embark on your own journey.

With any big leap, whether it's taking a new job or healing old wounds, there is a philosophical and practical side to things. There are motivations *and* methods to sift through. Here, I want to share a dozen "methods" or practical steps to consider when embarking on your journey.

1. Admit You Need Help

I remember exactly where I was when I admitted to myself that I wanted to change. It was New Year's Eve, my junior year of college. I was driving around town by myself going from party to party. I looked up and watched fireworks burst in the sky. "What am I doing?" I wondered. "There has to be more to life than this."

This was the beginning of the death of the old me and the birth of the new me. It was the beginning of me finding life to the fullest in Jesus Christ. Admitting your weakness and asking for help from others is one of the greatest signs of humility, one which the Lord will surely honor. There is power in saying, "I don't know where to go from here. Will you help me?"

Someone once said, "The Lord is a gentleman. He will rarely enter into someone's life without an invitation first." That night of humbly admitting I needed help was my way of inviting Him into my world. My life has never been the same since.

2. Find a Mentor

I didn't like it when other men gave me advice. That is until an older man started investing in me through a mentoring relationship. A mentor built a relationship with me and had the courage to tell me areas of my life that I didn't realize were having a negative impact on me. This never would have happened if I hadn't made the effort to find the mentor in the first place. When you submit to the authority of a mentor, God tends to show up in radical ways to honor your humility.

We've discussed this *ad nauseam*, but it's *that* important. I don't care how old you are, finding an older, mature person who you respect, and who will be honest with you can be hard to find. Oddly enough, discovering a good mentor is like dating: Find what you are looking for, and ask them to spend time with you.

I met William at a teacher training one summer day at one of our local high schools. William mentioned how he was a father, a mentor, a coach, and he loved Jesus. He asked good questions, and I enjoyed spending time with him. I emailed asking if he'd meet for breakfast. As our mentoring relationship grew, William and I met every month for the next five years.

When you find a godly man who is willing to invest in you, pursue them. Make it easy for them to spend time with you. Thank them often and honor their wisdom by doing what they say.

They are out there. Sometimes you just have to search high and low, but don't give up. If you get rejected, just move on to the next person. Fish in the right waters. Go to places where you are likely to find a good mentor. Bible studies and church small groups are good places to start. You can also ask your church leadership for recommendations. After you get to know them and begin to trust them, ask them to note things that they see in you that you may not see in yourself.

3. Embrace Self-reflection

Someone once said, "It's impossible to fix a moving vehicle." Rest, sabbath, and solitude can help usher you into something that very few people actually enjoy doing, and that's being self-reflective. Busyness often stands in the way, as does finding the time to do it. For many, the enemy lies to you and says rest and solitude are just code names for being lazy.

Self-reflection can be an extremely useful tool, but it sure is scary at the start. It's like cleaning out your closet. You know it'll be good to do it, but for some reason, you find it impossible to make time for it. For me, few things have helped me more than having a mentor guide me through an honest and objective inventory of myself. They asked questions like:

- Have you thought about how your past could be contributing to where you find yourself today?
- Why do you have a hard time trusting and forgiving people?
- What action steps are you going to pursue to become your best self?
- What is holding you back in life?
- What would a happy and free version of you look like?

Those questions stirred something in my heart. A major moment of reflection caused me to look inward and honestly assess where I was in life, and I was ready to admit that I didn't like who I was and that I was unhappy. Luckily, I was also in a stage of life where I was mature enough to do something about it.

Two things really helped me to self-reflect: quiet walks by myself and journaling. These helped me search my heart and find the answers to some of the bigger questions of life.

4. Embrace Feedback

Listening and receiving feedback can be difficult. Trusting that your friends or mentors are right and you are wrong can be even more challenging. Unknowingly, I protected myself from such feedback by never asking my mentors what they thought about events in my life.

One mentor called me out on that. A counselor by trade, Kyle, asks some of the best questions in town. I love meeting with him, and he gives me a lot to chew on through his wisdom. One day at our breakfast meeting, I was telling Kyle all about my life and what I planned on doing. Kyle just nodded and smiled as I talked. Then he hit me with this question.

"Zach, can I tell you something I have noticed?"

"Sure thing, Kyle. Anything," I said as I took a sip of my coffee.

"Well, we go out to breakfast and that's all good. But you never ask me what I think of your plans and actions. You just tell me what you're going to do instead of asking for my wisdom."

And he was right. Checking off the box that I met with a mentor is one thing. Actually requesting feedback and insight from them is another. It takes humility to receive the truth, but it is the truth that will help you become all God has for you.

If you are looking for a place to start, find someone that you trust, ask them out for coffee, and ask them if they'd be willing to help you by honestly answering a question or two. After they say yes, ask, "Are there any blind spots that you see that I don't?" and, "Do you see any yellow or red flags in my life that could keep me from being my best self?" Asking those questions takes some serious courage.

One thing to keep in mind: When you find a good mentor, he or she is committed to giving you honest feedback and has nothing to gain by lying to you. More times than not, that mentor wants the best for you and is willing to tell you the uncomfortable and hard truth. When they give you feedback, listen. Do not argue, justify, or minimize what they say. Ask them to help you find ways to grow and heal. They are not out to get you. You can trust them. Oftentimes, you'll need to chew on what they say, and a great place to do that is when you spend time with the Lord.

Lies from Satan, such as, "You're fine just the way you are," and, "How do you know that you can really change?" create obstacles in the middle of your journey. If this is something you are struggling with, try saying the lie you are wrestling with out loud or writing it down.

There is something about doing those two things that expose lies for what they are. You can also tell a friend or your mentor what's on your mind. Something as simple as "Sometimes I believe _____ about myself. What do you think about that?" can allow someone to help destroy the lies with truth. You can always fight against these lies by using the Word of God. Knowing who God says you are allows you to stand firm against the lies of Satan.

5. No One is Perfect

This is an important piece of advice when it comes to having a mentor; nobody's perfect. Even your mentor will disappoint you and possibly hurt you. Why? Because they are human. One of the most important mentors in my life had an affair and got divorced. Another one, a man who I had grown close to, chewed me out when I made a mistake.

We have to learn how to forgive people when they hurt us. We cannot carry offense. Proverbs 18:19 (PARA) says, "A brother offended is more unyielding than a strong city," and carrying offense lays the foundation of a bitter and hard heart.

Mentors may leave you before you're ready, or they may not show up when they said they would. I am confident the Lord gives mentors for a season to achieve an objective. Once their job is done, honor them and focus on all the good they did instead of the fact that they are leaving you. Mentors come and go, but the help and guidance they provide can impact you for a lifetime. Focus on the good, and let go of the bad. Give them grace and be thankful for what they did instead of focusing on what they didn't do.

6. Accepting the Honest Truth

I learned early on how to live my life in a state of constantly having to overcome. I figured I was doing a good enough job if I could just make it through each day on a good note. What I didn't think about, however, was how others were experiencing me while I was going through my issues.

This all came to a head one day when one of my employees told me she'd found a new job. I asked her why she was leaving, and she gave me a few surface-level answers. I was dumbfounded as to why she would leave, mainly because I thought all was going well. I called my board chairman, a man who was a seasoned businessman, to vent about the event.

I started off the conversation by telling him how ridiculous I thought my former employee was being and how she was making a poor decision. That's when my chairman intervened.

"Zach, can I tell you something?"

"Sure thing," I said.

"Well, I can tell you why she left. And if I were her, I would do the same thing. I've watched you at the office. You're a big guy, and you walk around with a scowl on your face most of the time. People are intimidated by you when you walk into the room. People have to walk on eggshells because they don't know which Zach they are going to get. I want to ask you a question, Zach, and I want you to think about this for a while: How do people experience you when you walk into a room?"

When I took the time to think about it, I had to accept the truth that my presence created an unsafe environment due to my insecurities from my past.

Facing issues from the past and confronting the reality that they are negatively impacting you and others around you can be a really hard thing to do. It's not easy to be honest with yourself about where you are and what you feel. No one likes to focus on their own shortcomings, but you must start the journey somewhere.

7. Fly with Eagles

I love my high school friends. They stuck by my side during some of the most difficult years of my life. That's why it was so hard when I realized I couldn't hang around them and be the man I wanted to be at the same time. I still loved them, called them often, and hung out with them during the daytime. But I knew I couldn't go out with them at night without regret.

My mentor, Steve Allen, says, "Eagles fly with eagles." This is his way of saying you are who you hang out with. In my late twenties, I decided to surround myself with people who I wanted to be like and made it a priority to be with them often to help guide me and encourage me. I realized that I couldn't make the change by myself, so I spent as much time as possible with these people. They were my support team.

Being intentional about who you hang out with is biblical. The Bible tells us to surround ourselves with wisdom, not foolishness. Deciding to stop hanging out with some of my best friends was one of the hardest decisions of my life, but it has been vital in helping me become who I am today. Choose your friends wisely. As the saying goes, "Show me your friends and I'll show you your future."

8. Just Do It

Like asking a girl out or jumping in the deep end of a swimming pool for the first time, there are some things in life that require you *to just do it*. Nike got it right. Asking for help is one of those things. And sometimes you have to ask someone for help as you take new steps forward. There is no magic potion that will help you make the first move. You have to just do it. More times than not, you'll find people are happy to help you out. Believe the best about people.

Asking for help is hard, and admitting you don't have it all together is harder, but the Lord is faithful to honor both acts of humility. Ask yourself, "How bad do I really want it?" Is your desire to improve greater than your desire to look like you have it all together? Have the guts to do whatever you have to do to overcome your obstacles.

9. Find a Church

I had no one to go with me to church when I first started attending regularly. It was hard and a little awkward. But it was a game changer. It was through the context of church that the Lord did so much in my heart. Finding a church home laid a foundation for what was to come.

It is important to find a local home church. Despite all its flaws, church is a place where you and other members can be committed to being known, serving each other, and impacting the world. Find a small group or a Bible study to help get to know people and to be known by others. Get to know your pastor, and allow them to shepherd you.

Going to church can be hard, specifically if you have no experience with church or have been hurt by the church. The church is full of broken people who will disappoint you, but it is the bride of Christ. No church is perfect, and you can nitpick what you like and don't like about it all day long. Just because the church is messy doesn't mean it's not necessary.

Do your homework to find a good fit for you, but the bottom line is that you just have to choose one, commit to it, start going, and start investing.

10. Take Sin Seriously

Have you ever seen a baby lion cub? It's just about the sweetest thing you've ever seen. They are fun to play with, cute as can be, and fairly harmless. But what happens when that lion cub grows up to be an adult? It can kill you in a matter of moments.

The same can be said with sin. At first, it seems harmless, a few drinks here and a glance at a pretty girl there. But when temptation starts to grow, it can take you out.

Something powerful happened the day I started taking my sin seriously. I became intentional about avoiding the pitfalls I had previously fallen into. For me, I knew I couldn't confront my drinking problem if I continued going to the bars a few times a week. I knew my lust issue wouldn't be resolved if I kept watching risqué movies and staying on the internet late at night. But I was too prideful to admit that I wasn't strong enough in those situations to come out clean on the other side.

I had to stop watching certain shows and listening to certain musicians. I took apps off my phone and was careful about how late I stayed out on the weekends. Some of my old friends made fun of me and said I was being extreme, but that's okay. The last time I checked, Jesus was pretty extreme about some things, too.

11. Be Real

"Everything is fine."

"I'm good."

"That didn't hurt."

Ever heard those words come out of a man's mouth?

In today's society, it is rare to find a person who is honest about how they are doing. Especially with men, there is a level of weakness in admitting that you aren't doing well. When you say all is well and nothing is wrong when you're going through a hard time, that's a lie. You are keeping those things hidden in the darkness instead of getting them into the light so that the Lord can heal them. It's okay to not be okay, and you are hurting yourself (and often those around you) by keeping your troubles to yourself. Share your struggles with people you trust. Talk about real issues instead of keeping it surface-level. Get the darkness out into the light, and watch the Lord honor your boldness.

12. Get Filled Up

The thing that ranks the highest in healing the father wound is spending daily, intentional time with God. To fight this battle well, we must be filled up with the Lord each day. His truth combats lies and gives us the armor we need to go out into this world. Each of us needs our Heavenly Father and His power. Every day, let Him remind you of who you are and who He is.

Busyness is an obstacle that can keep us stuck in our old patterns and prevent us from spending time with the Lord. All of us are busy, and there are a lot of things vying for our time. But you make time for what is important to you. Every good relationship requires time, effort, and intentionality to flourish—and your relationship with Jesus is no different.

Tell Me...

- Which practical step stands out to you the most? Why do you think that one stands out?
- Is there a step that you find challenging or one that you are avoiding? Is there one that you take issue with? Why do you think that is?
- Are there other practical methods for finding wholeness that you would add to this list? What do they look like?

CHAPTER 18

Boundaries and Honor

MAGINE YOU'RE A kid again. It's a summer night and you and your buddies decide to play a game of tag or hide and seek outside. What's the first question that pops up when preparing for the game?

What are the boundaries?

As humans, we seek boundaries. We crave clear markers for what is on and off limits. Whether it's a game of tag or a relational dynamic with family, we need clear dividing lines. Boundaries can be difficult, especially in a dysfunctional family where unhealthy patterns and dynamics have been around for a long time. Coming from a broken home, boundaries are essential in my relationship with a father who has hurt me in the past and a mother who struggles with codependency.

Dr. Henry Cloud in his book *Boundaries*, writes:

Boundaries define us. They define what is me and what is not me. A boundary shows me where I end and someone else begins, leading me to a sense of ownership. Knowing what I am to own and take responsibility for gives me freedom. Taking responsibility for my life opens up many different options.

Boundaries help us keep the good in and the bad out. Setting boundaries inevitably involves taking responsibility for your choices. You are the one who makes them. You are the one who must live with the consequences. And you are the one who may be keeping yourself from making the choices you could be happy with. We must own our own thoughts and clarify distorted thinking.[6]

A boundary is a line that marks the limit of something. It is a dividing line that says, "Here's where you stop. Please don't go any further." In relationships, boundaries can be really difficult because they are often not understood by the one who crosses your boundaries. If you have a close relationship with this person, coming up against a boundary can feel like a slap across the face. Questions arise. Confusion sets in. It can be difficult to navigate.

But here's the thing: You are an adult, and you have your own life to live. Things happened, and feelings were created due to the events of your past, and those feelings impact everything you do. Do whatever you have to do within biblical boundaries to give yourself the greatest opportunity to become all that the Lord has called you to be.

It doesn't matter how old you are, how mature you act, or how much money you have. You still have a heart that needs to be listened to and protected. Your heart is the wellspring of life. Take care of it so that you can be at your best.

So how do you set healthy boundaries and protect your heart, especially when you actively spend time around the father who hurt you? How do you honor him while setting boundaries that will help you protect your heart?

For me, it comes down to a few things:

1. Listen to your heart and the Holy Spirit. What bubbles up when you are around your father? How does his presence or interactions impact you and those around you? What does the Lord say about all of that, and where is the Holy Spirit leading you? If you know seeing your father is going to send you into a negative tailspin for weeks, maybe finding a better way to communicate with him would be a better alternative. Perhaps do a phone or video call every other week for a while instead of visiting.

    For years, seeing my father would send me into a rage. My inability to control my emotions would have most definitely had a negative effect on our relationship. I knew having a relationship with him was what the Lord had for me, but I had to build the relationship in my own time. God is not in a rush. For me, being patient and getting my heart right was necessary before I saw him face to face.

2. Create the environment you need to feel safe. When my father and I were first reconnecting, I only met with him in public restaurants, and I kept our interaction to about 90 minutes. I have heard of people inviting trusted friends or their spouses to meetings for moral support. You must do what you have to do to set yourself up for the best possible way to advance the relationship in a positive way. If that means meeting at a Denny's with your best friend by your side, so be it.

3. Clearly communicate what you want. A boundary line only works if the line itself is clearly visible to the other person. Clearly communicating exactly what you need is

a way to honor your dad during this process. Here's an example to follow:

A. State your desire: "Dad, I have been thinking about it a lot and I'd like to _____." Tell him what you want in the blank, whether it is talking on the phone or meeting in a public place. This gives the other person clarity on what you are trying to accomplish.

B. Set the boundary: "For me, the best way to do that is to _____." This is an opportunity to tell him where you'd like to meet and to let him know if someone else will be with you. By saying this, you are controlling the environment.

C. Reassure them of your desire: "I really want to make this happen, but I want you to know this is difficult for me. Communicating this way helps me set both of us up for success so that our relationship can grow stronger."

D. Put the ball in their court: "Is this something you are open to?" This question allows your father to say yes, no, or to make a suggestion. This is when the boundary is agreed upon by both parties.

I have found it extremely helpful to write out this conversation beforehand. This helps me stay on script and not give in to circumstances that are not good for me.

I can only do what the Lord asks me to do. I have no control over how my father responds. It is also helpful to limit my expectations and focus on what I can control. Letting go of expectations is a way of saying, "Lord, I trust You no matter what."

Know that it's okay to grieve during this process. What you're doing is hard. It's a weight you were never meant to carry. I knew the days leading up to interactions with my father and a few days after were going to be difficult for me. It helped to adjust my schedule accordingly and to let those whom I love know this is a tough week or two for me. Know that your heart will be stirred and emotions may be heightened. Find people to vent with or time to be alone. Try to explain to those closest to you what you're going through so that they can understand and support you.

Now, all of these pieces of the puzzle can be implemented with a father who has hurt you in the past. But what if he doesn't see it that way? How can you honor a father who chose to leave, is living in sin, and continues to feel like he was justified and did nothing wrong? How do you honor someone who is unrepentant and has hurt you in so many ways? How can you show grace to someone who is self-focused, immature, and prideful? On the other hand, what if other members of your family want to insist on acting like nothing happened? What if they want to act as if everything is okay?

For the person asking these questions in response to their father's actions, I applaud you. You are embarking on an extremely difficult journey.

This journey is considerably harder when the father you grew up with looks nothing like the father you have now. Perhaps your father was a good man when you were a child and was worthy of emulation, but now he is living a life of sin. When I was a child, we were in church every Sunday morning, Sunday night, and Wednesday night. When my father decided to leave, he pulled me aside and said, "Church is your choice now. You can choose if you want to go or not."

One day he was saying, "Faith is important. Let's try to be like Jesus." But the next week, it was like he was saying, "I'm going to do my thing, and you can do what you want to do. I'm done with this faith stuff." That's a really confusing message that can shake a kid's beliefs to the core.

Here comes the hard part: Honoring someone is a choice. They don't have to earn your honor. Just because you honor someone does not mean you approve of their behavior or choices. Honor simply means treating someone with respect, dignity, and not viewing them as less than you. It's the refusal to hold their actions against them in how you treat them. The crazy thing is sometimes you have to honor someone that you don't enjoy being around.

In this situation, I think of Jesus. How would He act in this set of circumstances? Would He badmouth or complain? Would He scream and shout or cut off the relationship? I don't think He would. But I don't think He would be all smiles and hugs either. I think He would love the sinner without condoning the sin. And I do think He would be sad. I think His heart would be broken at the state of your father's heart. I envision Him praying, asking the Father to fill Him up with what He needs to continue, and relying on the Holy Spirit to help Him through this tough time.

Acting like Jesus in the midst of an imperfect family, loving people unconditionally, and honoring those who have hurt you is one of the more difficult things we can do. And depending on the person and situation, it looks different for each of us. How you act and respond is one hundred percent between you and Jesus. Get with the Father and abide in His presence. I pray you receive clarity on how to respond and how to honor and that the Lord helps you give grace in the same way He has been gracious to you.

The truth is, boundaries are more than just a protective barrier for you. They are for your family and those under your care as well. To refuse to put them up is to put your family in harm's way. To reinforce them, however, is to steward your family with care.

Last holiday season, my wife and I decided we really wanted to focus on investing in our nuclear family. We wanted to start our own traditions with just our family of five. We thought of things to do each week leading up to Christmas, and we were getting excited about creating traditions for our kids.

Then my mother called and wanted to join in on our traditions as well. I had a choice to make. Do I ask my mom to come over, knowing she is lonely and wants more than anything to spend time with her grandkids? Or do I honor the commitment I made to my wife and limit these traditions to just our family of five?

I was stuck between a rock and a hard place.

Verses began to swirl in my head. "That is why a man leaves his father and mother and is united to his wife, and they become one flesh" (Genesis 2:24), came to mind. When talking about the family unit, Paul wrote, "Anyone who does not provide for their relatives, and especially for their own household, has denied the faith and is worse than an unbeliever" (1 Timothy 5:8). James wrote, "Religion that God our Father accepts as pure and faultless is this: to look after orphans and widows" (James 1:27).

Is my mother truly a widow? Is the 1 Timothy verse talking about providing emotionally, spiritually, or physically? Who comes first, my mother or my wife? Is it my responsibility to make sure that my mom doesn't feel lonely, or is it up to her to meet her own needs? How do I love my wife well and lead my family while ensuring that I am honoring my mother as well, knowing that she is all alone and needy?

These are all questions I do not know the answer to.

It is here that I must set clear boundaries for the sake of the one I am called to love first: my wife. I must also set boundaries to help me be the best version of myself for my wife and kids and to help my mom meet her own needs. I need to keep in mind that my mother is an adult and is fully capable of finding people to help her not feel lonely. While her life may not have turned out how she thought it would, that doesn't mean all is lost. She can still make the most of a tough situation. If my mom is looking to anyone else besides Jesus to fulfill her, including me, it's just not going to work out. Only He can heal her hurts and provide peace and comfort.

Here's another problem—I cannot help but feel pain and a little sadness because I *do* want to help. I cannot help but want to be "the savior" and give my mom all of her desires. But when I tried to serve my mom *and* wife, it left both parties unfulfilled and me exhausted.

So, I focus on doing my best to lead my wife and children and give them the best family experience possible, while doing my best to love my mom and be there for her as much as I can under a clear set of boundaries. I make efforts to include her when it is healthy for my nuclear family. When disappointments arise and I don't meet my mother's expectations or standards, I will apologize and leave it at that. I am going to set clear, healthy boundaries, and I am going to honor my mother in a way that I can stand before God knowing I treated my mother well in the midst of a hard situation.

Caring for a wife, a family, and a single mother is complicated. There is no "one right way" to do it. It is a dance. It is a product of a broken world. There are different seasons and degrees of interaction. It is not fair, it is not fun, but we can do everything in our power to honor God through it.

Boundaries are not cruel but kind. They are not optional but necessary. They are not cynical but safe. If you haven't already, begin to draw yours. Diving back into interaction with someone who has hurt you takes a certain amount of risk. While you will never remove that risk completely, you can mitigate it through a clear set of boundaries for you and yours.

Tell Me...

- Is honoring your mother or father something that comes easily to you? If not, please share why you think that is the case. If so, how do you show honor to them?
- Have you ever had to choose between your mother, father, and spouse or kids? How did you handle that?
- What kind of boundaries have you set with your family? Are there any boundaries that you need to set for the health of yourself or your nuclear family?

CHAPTER 19

The Common Inquiries

ONE OF MY joys in life is encouraging other men in the name of Jesus. Whether it is encouraging other middle-aged fathers or discipling young men in their twenties, somehow the topic of fathers always comes up. Unfortunately, oftentimes we have similar stories regarding being raised in a broken family. Once they find out that I, too, come from a family like theirs, the questions start flying. And they're always the same questions.

"It's complicated."

That's my go-to phrase regarding most things that involve my father and processing my pains.

Toss in kids and it gets even more messy. It's not easy to explain why you have four thanksgivings, why mom has a different last name than you, and why your extended family is quite different from your friends.

Throughout my years of ministry, a few questions about dealing with a father wound tend to surface more than others. This chapter is my attempt to answer those questions because they might be yours as well.

Now, let me be really clear from the beginning: The answers are simply my experiences with these particular inquiries. I do not have all of the answers and never will. Most of these questions do not have a "one size fits all" answer to them, as each family is different. Every person is different. And there is more than one way to find success as you address these questions. As you read this chapter:

1. I hope these questions put words to your feelings and the situation when and if you are having a hard time articulating them out loud.
2. I hope and pray you find comfort in knowing you are not alone in wondering these same things.
3. I hope and pray these answers help you find wholeness and healing, and to extend forgiveness while also honoring your father to whatever extent possible.

And above all, I hope addressing these questions helps you gain a little ground in your father wound journey.

Will things ever be normal?

Just because I have forgiven my father doesn't mean all is normal. Coming to terms with the fact that my family isn't like healthier families has helped me in several ways, the main one being I have stopped comparing. I see it as having two options: I can either be mad because I don't have the ideal family or give grace amid the dysfunction and adjust my mindset and expectations.

I can give grace when people aren't perfect and don't behave how I want them to one hundred percent of the time. I can give grace to myself for not handling every situation the way Jesus would, and I can be okay with the fact that I'm doing the best that I can in this season.

For me, a better question is, "What am I okay with?" No family is normal. We all have our quirks and dysfunctions because we are all broken in one way or another. Add in step-siblings, half-siblings, and step-parents, and things can get weird quickly.

Find a relationship dynamic that both you and your father are okay with and go from there. My father knows I'll probably see him and his new family once, maybe twice a year. We talk on the phone every six weeks or so. That's good for us. It works. Is it perfect? No. But that's okay. Very few things in life are perfect.

How do I bring up fond childhood memories that involve my parents without causing negative emotions?

The mind is a funny thing. Simple daily actions can trigger memories from my past. Just the other day, I was having some back pains. I asked my oldest son to walk on my back and put some pressure on the areas of pain. As he got on my back, a memory of me walking on my dad's back flashed in my mind. *I wasn't expecting that*, I thought. Years ago, that memory could have ruined my night. But I have figured out a few things that have helped me stay in a positive mindset.

1. Involve the Helper: Whenever a memory arises that causes me to pause, I take it to the Lord as soon as I can. Usually, it involves bringing the situation up during my quiet times with the Holy Spirit. It is there I can ask questions like, "Why did that trigger me?" or, "Why did I react the way I did when that memory popped up?" This gives the Holy Spirit an opportunity to guide us through what is going on in our hearts. It gives you an opportunity to process and helps you heal.

   I tend to compare the pains of my past to the thorn in Paul's side in 2 Corinthians 12:7-10: "Therefore, in order to keep me from becoming conceited, I was given a thorn in my flesh, a messenger of Satan, to torment me. Three times I pleaded with the Lord to take it away from me. But he said to me, 'My grace is sufficient for you, for my power is made perfect in weakness.' Therefore I will boast all the more gladly about my weaknesses, so that Christ's power may rest on me. That is why, for Christ's sake, I delight in weaknesses, in insults, in hardships, in persecutions, in difficulties. For when I am weak, then I am strong."

The Holy Spirit is called the Helper. He is the Father of Compassion and the Great Comforter. When the hurts pop up, allow the Lord and God's people to support and guide you as you travel this journey to wholeness and forgiveness. It's also an opportunity to direct our attention to Jesus. May the failures of our parents lead us to praise the perfection of God.

2. Process your Feelings: Having a safe place to engage your heart and really understand what is going on in your soul is essential to dealing with negative emotions. It is important to identify your feelings and deal with them in a timely manner. If you neglect them, the emotions bubbling up may very well turn into a gushing geyser that erupts under pressure.

There are many ways to sort out your feelings and there is no wrong way to do it. Feel free to do whatever works for you. Journaling, taking a walk, praying, or talking to a trusted friend or counselor are all things that help me to process. It is during these times that I can truly bring my feelings to Jesus and allow the Holy Spirit to comfort me on this journey. I can trade my sorrow for contentment and my pain for peace.

3. Beware of the spiral of negativity: From time to time, we can all fall into the trap of asking questions that have no answer. "Why did this happen to me?" "What would have happened if this _____ happened?" Or, "I wonder how

my life would be different if my upbringing was healthy?" These are all questions that I have asked myself at one time or another. The bad thing about these questions is they never do any good. In fact, they just seem to make things worse. They have no answer and satisfaction won't come from asking them.

I remember a time in my life when I was confronted with the reality that my father wound always did one of two things to me: It `caused me to ignore my emotions and push them down deep in my soul, or it caused me to become introspective and "what if" myself into a dark place. Both of those experiences are not good. But I learned how to keep myself from going to those two places. When I felt myself experiencing hurt or anger, I dealt with it as soon as possible and didn't allow myself to ask unproductive questions, simmering in pain. As soon as I realized I was going down the spiral of asking these questions, I simply said to myself, "Stop. These are doing no good," and would change my thinking quickly.

No matter how much your childhood experiences negatively impacted you, try focusing on the good memories you have. There are always things you can be thankful for, even in the midst of hardships. It is important to look back on the good times that brought joy into your life. But this takes a little bit of work. Allowing the Holy Spirit to lead you, processing your emotions in a healthy way, and avoiding negative thinking can keep the enemy from robbing you of the good memories so that you can be thankful for what the Lord has done in your life.

How do I take a stand against the generational curse of divorce without making my parents feel like a failure?

A parent who has a failed marriage may feel just like that—a failure. Defensiveness may come as they feel shame or guilt about what has happened. Shame may rear its ugly head as well, which can make a person act in all sorts of ways. Fear of disappointing their children or embarrassment over what people could be saying or thinking may also be playing a part in how they are acting.

Now, what I am about to ask you to consider is hard—it is asking you to stand in the middle of possible hurt and anger and act like Jesus. I believe this is an opportunity for you to model compassion. Have you ever felt like a failure before? Have you ever experienced guilt, shame, or embarrassment? It's not fun. This is a chance to show mercy and grace. To love the person even amid sin or a bad decision. To say, "I don't love the choice you made nor do I agree with you, but I love you." I've seen this go as well as it could when both parties agree to disagree. I've also seen it kill relationships when the parent doesn't understand why you aren't taking their side. Regardless, the only things you can control are your heart and your efforts to communicate in an honorable way. Your parent's response is up to them.

Loving someone while not seeing eye to eye is a difficult concept. Staying in relationship when you disagree with their words and actions takes an act of maturity on your part. It's okay to disagree. It's perfectly within your rights to voice your opinion that you wish things were different. It's also the choice of your parent to own their reaction to your opinion. But it's also our call as followers of Jesus to honor our parents and be peacemakers. Matthew 5:9 says, "Blessed are the peacemakers," and Romans 12:18 says, "If possible, so far as it depends on you, live peaceably with all."

When I look back on hard situations or difficult conversations, I always want to be able to say with one hundred percent integrity, "I did all I knew to do to make this situation turn out well. There isn't one more thing I could have done. I acted like Jesus to the best of my ability." As much as it depends on you, live a life where you have no regrets in your relationships.

How do I balance quality time during special events and holidays when my parents can't stand being in the same room?

We were getting ready for Thanksgiving, preparing the turkey, and cleaning the house, when my son said, "Hey Dad, is Papa coming to Thanksgiving?" I looked at him and gently said, "No, son, not this year." Truth is, my son has never spent a major holiday with my father, and that's really unfortunate on multiple fronts.

This is a hard one. How do you choose which parent comes to which event? Even harder, if you have children, how do you explain why Grandma can come to your birthday party or Christmas dinner, but Grandpa can't? There is no simple answer here. The best wisdom I can give is this: Consider your heart, what your spouse thinks, what your kids think, and then make the best decision you can. Do what is best for your family. Some may say you should be fair, and I can see the logic in that. Feel free to go in that direction if it is best for your family.

For me, my father chose to leave my family, decided to get remarried and start afresh with his new family. My mom is single and all alone. Those circumstances definitely play a part in who comes to what. My children love both my mom and my dad, which also impacts the choices I make. I also know that being around my biological family, with all of our history and hurts, tends to, unfortunately, bring out the worst in me. Knowing that, I keep the visits short and sweet. I probably won't be going on week-long vacations with either parent anytime soon, and that's okay. I have to remember that I am doing the best that I can. It is not a simple decision to make. It is complicated.

It is your family. You set the rules. People may not agree with your choice, or like it, but you can choose to do what is best for you and those closest to you.

Will it ever hurt less?

I was riding in the car with my friend, Jeff. Jeff is a 50-something-year-old father of six older kids. He was telling me his son was thinking of transferring schools and asked for advice. Jeff mentioned bringing up some points with his boy that he likely hadn't considered—advising him to take a day and pray about it. His son came back the next day and said, "I thought about what you said, Dad. I think you're right. I am going to stay where I am."

It was a simple story, nothing special. But as Jeff finished the story, I stared off in the distance and thought, *So, that's what it is like to have a father speak into your life....* And just like that, my father wound opened up again.

Unforeseen conversations or situations like that happen all the time. James 1:12 came to mind, "Blessed is the one who perseveres under trial because, having stood the test, that person will receive the crown of life that the Lord has promised to those who love him."

I wonder from time to time if it will ever hurt less. While there is likely no "getting over it," there is a better perspective that's available. I can grow in how I think about it. For example, in my mid-twenties, the conversation I had with Jeff would have sidelined me for days. My anger and bitterness would have negatively impacted all that I did. Fast-forward 20 years later, and it only distracted me for a moment.

So yes, the hurt can become less.

I cannot control being exposed to circumstances, conversations, or topics that remind me of my hurt, but I can use them as a gauge to see how my heart is doing. If negative emotions pop up, it is my heart's way of telling me that I need to do something. Maybe I need to forgive some more. Perhaps I need to take some time to process by myself or with a trusted friend. Or maybe I just need to mourn and grieve the fact that my family was broken by sin.

The more effort and intentionality you put into healing your heart and overcoming your past, the less it will hurt. I believe you can overcome this and deal with your pain in a healthy way. And God will be with you through it all. Psalm 34 says, "God is near to the brokenhearted." God also wants you to be free from chronic emotional pain.

Remember that God is not in a hurry when it comes to your healing. He will wait to give you the next step when your heart is ready. Patience is needed as your healing journey is not a race. There are even seasons of rest as you don't always have to push through and deal with your pain.

Years ago, when I read the "With God, all things are possible" verse in Matthew 19:26, it would make me angry. If all things are possible, then God should just make this pain go away, right? But now I realize that pain isn't always a bad thing. C. S. Lewis writes in his book, *The Problem of Pain*, "God whispers to us in our pleasures, speaks in our conscience, but shouts in our pains. [Pain] is His megaphone to rouse a deaf world." God may not make our pain go away in short order, but maybe He will use it to bring us closer to Him and to help us know ourselves better. And that is a great gift.

The Apostle James famously wrote, "Consider it pure joy, my brothers and sisters, whenever you face trials of many kinds, because you know that the testing of your faith produces perseverance. Let perseverance finish its work so that you may be mature and complete, not lacking anything" (James 1:2-4). It really is possible that one day, you will look back at the pain you've endured and realize it has given you perspective, maturity, wisdom, and compassion. It is possible that your pain, and the healing of it, have turned you into the best version of yourself.

How do I balance the needs of my wife with the needs of my single mother?

What do you do when the two most important people in your life have conflicting needs? What do you do when your mother has a desire to spend Christmas Eve with you, but your wife has a desire to spend that precious night together as a nuclear family? Maybe your mom wants to come over every week for Sunday lunch and your wife is not okay with it. That's called a lose-lose. Someone that you love dearly is going to be hurt and rejected no matter the decision that you make. It is in moments like these that I realize just how truly broken this world is.

The fact that my mom is alone is an absolutely heartbreaking reality. The fact that she does not have a husband to support her and give her the companionship that we all want is probably not how she thought her life would end up. Unfortunately, sometimes those needs and expectations can get passed on to you.

Oftentimes, I have felt the pressure to meet my mother's every need. I have tried to play the role of husband and son. I try to make sure that she does not feel lonely and alone. The bad part is, in the midst of trying to take care of my mom, I put her needs above the needs of my wife. That's not a good thing. My wife should be my number one priority, even over the needs of my mom.

How do I explain this to my wife? How do I explain this to my mom? I'm afraid someone is going to be hurt or angry at me, even though I am just trying to make everyone happy. But here's the reality. You can't make everyone happy. This is an unfortunate situation with no clear winners. You might have to absorb the pain from your mom. You may have to disappoint here. Tough conversations must be had with both your mother and your spouse.

When I find myself in these situations, I try to do the following:

- Accept the fact that this is a terrible situation. Allow your heart to feel the brokenness of this world, which helps you respond compassionately.
- Remain calm and figure out how to have productive conversations. Clearly understand the needs of both parties.

- Prioritize my wife by setting healthy boundaries. Communicate this to my mother in a gentle way.
- Trust that the Lord loves my mom more than I do. Trust that He is bigger than this situation. Remind myself that I am not my mom's savior; only the Lord can do that.
- Find an older, trusted confidant or counselor to give me wisdom in the situation.

I will not pretend that I do this well every time. Situations like these are some of the hardest moments that I have ever faced. All I can do is do the best I can, and I have to be okay with that. It's moments like these that I need as much of the grace of God as possible.

How do I talk truthfully to young kids about complicated family situations without vilifying anyone unnecessarily?

"Wait a minute," my son said from the back seat, looking confused. "So, you're telling me that Nana and Papa used to be married?"

"That's right, son. Now who wants ice cream?" I said, trying to change the subject as quickly as I could.

"And now Papa is married to Gram...?" my son prodded.

How do you share the truth without jading your child's view of their grandparent? It's a delicate situation, that's for sure. Sharing your family history with your children can be complicated at best and it is different for each family. There are many factors to consider such as timing, maturity, and past situations. The reality is your child will find out what happened sooner or later, so you can control the narrative to a certain degree by being intentional in sharing what happened in a safe environment. This is far better than your children discovering family drama or trauma from another source.

For me, I see the situation as a giant jigsaw puzzle that is going to take a long time to complete. Each season my child grows more mature, I give them a new piece to the puzzle. When they are really young, I keep the stories of the past high level. As they get older the story may change from, "Papa and Nana had a hard time getting along" to "Papa and Nana got divorced, and now Papa is married to Gram." Perhaps when they are adults and able to understand negative actions and hard situations while still loving the person, I will share with them the full story.

It is important that no one vilifies the other person during this process. The last thing your children need is to hear Nana talking bad about Papa and vice versa. Your father could have been an absent father but is a wonderful grandfather. You don't want your past experiences to keep your child from experiencing the blessing of a positive adult in their life. After all, Proverbs 17:6 says, "Grandchildren are the crown of the aged." What an excellent opportunity we have as children to give our fathers a chance at redemption with their grandchildren while obviously keeping in mind the safety of the child first and foremost.

While this is awkward and hard to navigate, it is an opportunity to speak to your children about marriage and paint a picture of a healthy one. Share with them that a healthy marriage takes a lot of communication, compromise, and forgiveness. The topic can give your children a chance to ask questions to further learn about their family and the concept of marriage. You can share your thoughts on the topic and hopefully, they will walk away having learned a thing or two.

It's up to you to tell the story of your past in your own timing, but I do encourage you to broach the topic sooner or later. Do not stuff the past down deep and never talk about it. That's no good for anyone and the kids will notice. Engage the Lord and your spouse and decide how to share bits and pieces of the story in an appropriate way and at the right time.

* * *

How can I walk in maturity in my relationship with my parents?

Typically, I am the one initiating a relationship with my father. I reached out and started the forgiveness process. I call and set up trips to see him and his family. I do the majority of the outreach. Why is that? I thought initiating a relationship was the job of the parent.

I feel like if I stopped trying, my relationship with my father would slowly disintegrate and somehow it would be my fault. Why do I have to be the mature one when my father caused all of this by his actions? That question is very dangerous and probably the one I thought about the most when thinking about my family. If I am not careful, that question will lead me to anger, bitterness, and removing myself from the relationship.

Like most of the questions in this chapter, the answer is simply that you sometimes just have to do the right thing because that's what God calls you to do. If I did whatever I wanted to do all of the time, my life would probably end up being pretty miserable. I continue to pursue my father because honoring him honors God. I care way more about what God thinks of me than what my father thinks of me.

It all comes down to faith. I believe and trust that if I do what God calls me to, that is what is best for me. I believe if I do the right thing and honor my father, even though it is incredibly difficult, then my actions will honor and glorify God. He will look at my heart and say, "Well done, good and faithful servant." Loving and pursuing an imperfect parent is something God can use to help us grow in maturity and Christlikeness. Proverbs 16:4 says, "The Lord has made everything for his own purposes, even the wicked for a day of disaster." Don't lose sight of God's purpose amidst your pain.

After all, Paul wrote, "And we know that in all things God works for the good of those who love him, who have been called according to his purpose" (Romans 8:28). God is up to something good, but it is our choice to join Him in the process. The painting may not make sense while it is being painted, but I have confidence one day you will step back and see the beauty God created out of a mess.

Tell Me...

- Which question do you relate to the most?
- Name a time that you felt like you had to grow up too fast or be the mature one in your family. What did that look like?

PART FOUR

Proclaim

CHAPTER 20

The Turning

THERE ARE TIMES in my journey of overcoming my father wound when I wonder if the process will ever end. There are periods where I felt I was making major progress and other times when it felt like I hadn't moved forward at all. There are seasons when I want to quit. It seemed I had nothing else to give and was defeated after trying everything I knew to do, yet had nothing to show for it.

My father wound still pops up from time to time, and that is totally normal. It seems with each season of my life, a new level of depth and meaning arises from my father wound. The seasons when it felt like nothing was happening were times when God was preparing me for what was next. Virtues like patience, perseverance, and endurance were being instilled during those times. God had a plan for me and this process was part of it. The Lord has a track record of using trials and tribulations to accomplish His plans for those He loves (see Romans 8:28).

One of my favorite stories in the Bible is of Joseph, which can be found in Genesis 37-50. I like this area of Scripture because I can relate to it. Joseph endured awful things in his life, things that would have made most people tap out and quit. But he endured and God turned those terrible events into a miracle that saved and gave hope to His people for generations to come.

All in all, everything Joseph went through lasted around 13 years. For over a decade, he had to face the fact that his family betrayed him, he was sold into slavery, falsely accused, and sent to prison, and his friends in prison forgot about him. I'd say Joseph was dealt a pretty terrible hand in the game of life. But Joseph never gave up. He always trusted that God would turn this bad into good.

And finally, it happened. Joseph was released from prison and found favor with the king. He quickly rose the ranks in Egypt and became governor over all the land, finding a way to feed the entire nation and lead them through the worst famine Egypt had ever seen. The Lord not only turned Joseph's nightmare into a happy ending, but He abundantly blessed Joseph and used his life to bless many, many people.

It was the journey that made the man. Joseph could have quit at any time, throwing in the towel and cursing God in anger, but he didn't. He stayed faithful to the Lord. That's why he was able to boldly say to his brothers when he forgave them, "You meant evil against me, but God meant it for good."

The common thread in Joseph's life is that he lived a life of export. Whether he was in the palace or in the prison, he continued to export the things that God had imported into him. He shared, proclaimed, and lived in generosity, despite his circumstances, and got back what the enemy stole.

Satan uses what happened to you and your father to destroy you. But, like God did for Joseph, the Lord can turn your situation from bad to good. He can take what Satan used for evil and turn it into good—and not just for you, but for future generations too.

The enemy will do whatever he can to kill the process, but don't fall into his traps. Enlisting a support system to help you out when the going gets tough is vital. Surround yourself with people who can pick you up when you fall. Continue to bear in mind that this whole thing is bigger than one trial or one bad season—it's about the proclamation of the goodness of God.

Not only did the enemy cause you pain, but he will actively work to disrupt your process of healing from that pain. Where God wants to make a bad situation whole, Satan wants to make a bad situation worse.

In 2 Kings 4, there is a widow who is in quite a predicament. Her husband had died. When he died, the household income dried up. This was a particularly painful scenario because they had outstanding debt. With no means of repaying that debt, her two sons were taken into slave labor in order to pay it off.

Think of it: She was already dealing with the loss of her husband. To compound the fracture, her kids are then taken from her to become slaves. Talk about a bad situation becoming worse.

Fortunately, God had a miracle in mind. Elisha shows up and asks the widow what she has in the house. Turns out, she has nothing but a little jar of oil. Apparently, this was more than enough for God to work with. You may not feel like you have much at your disposal. Rest assured, it's enough for God to work to turn your situation around.

Elisha tells the widow to go collect empty vessels. She does. He then tells her to pour out the little jar of oil that she has into all of the vessels. On a human scale, the math doesn't add up. On God's scale, it does. As she tips the jar, the oil is multiplied, and she is supernaturally able to fill all of the vessels.

She sells the jars of oil, buys her sons back from slavery, and has leftover money to live on.

The turning around of her situation did cost her something. She had to do the illogical. She had to get busy increasing her capacity by collecting oil. She had to step out in obedience when it didn't make sense to the human mind.

It took sacrifice.

When I got serious about making Jesus the Lord of my life, I decided to start making some sacrifices. I sacrificed my two biggest resources, time and money, to put myself in situations to grow in my walk with the Lord. I woke up early to spend time with Him, sacrificing my dearly beloved sleep. I went to conferences, retreats, and events to grow in my faith.

In my life, I have found that the Lord honors sacrifices that cost you things that are important to you. It's your way of saying, "Lord, I want You more than I want these other things." Do the things that cost you something, and watch the Lord turn things in your life around.

Forgiveness, as we discussed earlier in the book, is a special kind of sacrifice. You are sacrificing the comfort of your old buddy named resentment. For me, I had to *choose* to forgive my father. It was not some warm, bubbly, spontaneous eruption of love. If I hadn't taken action, I'm not sure we ever would have spoken again. Choosing to forgive even when the other party thinks they made no mistake is a difficult and mature move. Forgiveness is a choice and one that only you can make.

Depending on your story, choosing to forgive can be one of the most courageous things you can ever do. By choosing to forgive, you are taking the weight off your shoulders and placing it squarely on the shoulders of Jesus. Make the choice to forgive. Get free.

Let's face it, you could make a bunch of really positive changes in your life, but if the sacrifice of forgiveness is not offered, you will seriously inhibit your progress.

Consider writing a letter to your father. This is an especially good exercise if you do not know where your father is or if he has passed away. If you do have access to him, it is up to you to give the letter to him or not, but just the act of writing the letter can help you process your heart and your feelings in a powerful way.

Writing brings clarity. As you face a blank page and begin to unpack with written words, you will likely find it to be therapeutic. For many, this is a turning point in their journey. A big part of processing pain is proclaiming it, so by opening up and putting things on paper, you may just find breakthrough.

As I look back on my father wound journey, I can see all the Lord did along the way. He strengthened me through ups and downs, and He guided me all along the way. He proved to me that He was a good Father and provided people to support me when times were tough. Like Joseph, I could have quit at any time. I'm sure glad I didn't.

It is one thing to change your actions, but a whole different ball game when you talk about changing your heart. It is hard work to search your heart to reveal sins that are keeping you in bondage. We aren't looking for behavior modification, but instead a desire to want to please the Lord with our words and actions. Heart change takes a while in most cases. Stay in the process and trust that the Lord is working, even if you can't feel it.

As you confront your father wound head-on, I am confident you too will say, "It was worth it" when your journey comes to a close.

Tell Me...

- What positive qualities, lessons, or experiences has your father wound produced in your life?
- When the chapter mentioned the need to make personal sacrifices, did anything come to mind?
- What would you say if you wrote your father a letter?
- Has the enemy used your father wound to try and kill you? How so?

CHAPTER 21

But God

THE DAY I met Larry all those years ago, God set me on fire for Him and completely changed my life. I look back at who I was and I barely recognize that man. Now, I am a husband, father, and a man who seeks first the Kingdom of God. I run a ministry that supports single mothers and helps kids who grow up without a father figure present. I have a good relationship with my father and am surrounded by people who love and support me.

When I find out someone has the same story as me, I see it as an opportunity to help set that person free. If God can give me freedom and restoration, He can do the same for you.

Restoration means *to heal or repair*. Think of new skin that grows over a wound over time; that's restoration. Our God is a God of restoration, which I have experienced first-hand. And I'm not the only one who has experienced His restorative power.

- Moses killed a man, but God restored him and used him to lead His people out of Israel.

- David committed adultery, but God called him a "man after God's own heart."
- Paul used to kill Christians, but God used him to advance the Kingdom in some major ways.
- Peter denied Jesus three times when he was needed most, but God said he would be the rock upon which the church was built.

You get the point.

The Bible says that God will restore the years the locusts have eaten and He will replace it with plenty, satisfying us in the process (see Joel 2:25-27). He declares health will be restored and wounds will be healed (see Jeremiah 30:17). The Psalms declare that God will restore our soul and lead us in paths of righteousness (see Psalm 23:3).

This is the heartbeat of God the Father.

Notice, the passage in Joel deals with God restoring things around us, Jeremiah speaks of God restoring things upon us (physical healing), and the Psalms declare the restoration of things *within* us.

As I really take a moment to ponder that truth, it is almost too much for me to handle. The Lord takes all my junk, all my sin, past and present, and removes it. Nothing I have done is too much for Him. He makes all things new—my heart, my relationships, my mind.

One could live on these promises forever. But it gets better. In Ephesians 2:1-10, a favorite area of Scripture for me, Paul puts the icing on the cake, effectively saying that you and I were dead in our trespasses and sins. We followed the course of the world and said "yes" to the enemy's wishes. But God, being rich in mercy and unmatched love, brought us to life with Christ, right there in the midst of our sin and shame. We were saved, not by efforts, works, performance, or by being good boys and girls. No, it was by grace alone. And how did we access that grace? Simple faith. In that exchange, we were raised up to be seated at the throne with Jesus, prepared to carry out our unique callings and purposes (see Ephesians 2:1-10).

We were dead, but then God showed up. We were a mess, but then God cleaned us up. And it had nothing to do with me, and it has nothing to do with you.

Now that's grace. That's a good Father.

Redemption is different from restoration. Restoration is about healing and redemption is about freedom. To redeem is to deliver from something or to set a person free. It means to loosen the chains of bondage and to buy back something that was lost. And that's exactly what Jesus Christ did on the cross. He paid the price of death to buy my freedom from sin.

Growing up, I heard the "Jesus died on the cross for my sins" talk thousands of times. I thought, "A guy died for all of us to forgive our sins. I guess that's cool." But it never really hit home with me until I took the time to make the death of Jesus a personal event. Instead of thinking, "Jesus Christ died for mankind," I thought, "Jesus Christ died for me, Zach Garza. He died to set me free from the pains of my childhood and the sins I committed then and now. He died to loosen the chains of self-hatred, anger, and bitterness. He came to set me free from hurt and pain and to replace it with a never-ending, unconditional love."

To make the crucifixion personal meant to imagine making eye contact with Jesus Christ on the cross and hearing Him say, "I am doing this because I love you. It is my joy to set you free." For God so loved the world, He gave His one and only Son.

The Bible is clear about what God thinks of redemption. He says we have redemption through the blood of Jesus. He says we have redemption, which forgives all our sins.

- Ephesians 1:7: "In him we have redemption through his blood, the forgiveness of our trespasses, according to the riches of his grace."

- Colossians 1:14: "In whom we have redemption, the forgiveness of sins."
- Isaiah 44:22: "I have blotted out your transgressions like a cloud and your sins like mist; return to me, for I have redeemed you."

How kind of God the Father to restore and redeem us. Not only does He love and take care of His children, but He sets them up for success as well—to overcome that which is holding them back from all He has and all He created them to be.

Having children of my own really helped me understand God the Father in a new way. It helped me solidify the fact that God is *for* me. He is on my side. He wants me to succeed. This hit me one day as I watched my four-year-old son play basketball. My son, along with most kids his age, isn't what I would call a coordinated or skilled basketball player. He just runs around the court looking lost. It's actually pretty cute. As a father, I found myself caring a ton about how my son was doing. I wanted, deep down in my heart, for him to have fun, score points, and make friends. This was a legitimate desire of mine. When he got the ball, I cheered for him. When he messed up, I encouraged him. After the game, win or lose, I hug him and we celebrate together.

That's exactly how God the Father is with you and me at all times. He is for us. He wants us to succeed. He wants us to become all that He created us to be.

I believe that God has a "But God" moment for you today, for the Lord loves to rewrite the narrative of your life. When it comes to rewriting the story of your life, God has a major part to play, but so do you. You're the main character in the story. God wants to work with you, as opposed to you sitting on the sidelines and watching. God gives you every opportunity to be made new, and He is patient in waiting for you.

One day, when you are old and talking to your children and they ask you to tell them the story of your life, I pray the Lord works in such a way that you will be able to say, "I grew up without a father in my life and that left me with some pretty tough circumstances, *but God*..."

Your Pain Redeemed

The Lord has a beautiful way of using the pain of someone else to impact the world in a positive way. People's lives very rarely are without complication—things such as food shortages, lack of education, or situations of abuse are just a few examples. But, when someone overcomes obstacles in their life, they often take the tools it took to overcome that obstacle and use them as a gift to give to others who are going through similar situations.

For example, a person who is a recovering alcoholic is more likely to comfort a person struggling with alcoholism because he knows what he is going through. Single mothers know what it is like to raise a child on their own and can help the newly single moms be better supported and encouraged because they know the struggle firsthand. God can use your experience for good by providing an example to look up to for someone in need or going through something similar. Your presence alone is an encouragement saying, "I've been where you are and I've overcome. If I can, you can too." You give hope, and there is nothing more powerful to a person who is struggling than the simple force of *hope*.

God uses your pain to create a fire in you to help others like you. More on that in the chapter to follow. For me, God took a kid who grew up without a father figure to now help kids who are in the same situation as I was through a mentor relationship, a father-figure type person for them to emulate. When I see a kid growing up without a father, I can feel what he or she is feeling. There is nothing else in this world that my heart burns so passionately for than helping those impacted by the father wound to overcome their pain.

This passion did not come from a random idea. It came from deep pain. Spurred by my past, the Lord turned my pain into passion, my trauma into triumph.

Tell Me...

- Do you have a "but God" moment? "I was _____, but God_____."
- What particular areas of pain and struggle has God brought you out of? How might you be specially equipped to help others in that same trap?
- Has your "pain turned into passion" in any area of your life?

CHAPTER 22

Becoming What You Never Had

NOW THAT MY kids are older, I am acutely aware of how much they watch and emulate me. Everything I do, they do. I find them repeating phrases I say often. The days are long, but the years are short, and I want to maximize the season.

I want more than anything to become what I never had as a child. I don't want my kids to know a day when they didn't have full confidence in the love of their father. The trick is, how do I do that if I have never had that in my own life? How can I become what I never saw?

For those with father wounds, breaking the generational cycle within your own family takes intentional, prayerful, and hard work, but can be done. By no means do I have it all figured out, as each season brings about a new set of challenges and celebrations, but I want to share important things I have learned from other men as I have become a spouse, father, and role model for my kids. Here is a list of practical to-dos I have learned from mentors, friends, and other father figures.

For Your Spouse

My wife is the most important human being in my life. The most important thing you can give your children is a healthy marriage and a healthy spouse. If mom and dad are doing well, more often than not, the kids will follow. Here are some things that I have learned from others to make sure I am being a loving spouse to my bride:

Laugh Often: I am amazed at my ability to be all business whenever I get home. Sometimes I am so concerned with dishes and work and kids and dinner that I forget to bring joy into my home. One thing I do before I walk into the door is sit in my car and let go of all that happened during the workday. I release all worry, anxiety, and thoughts and leave them in the car. I then put a smile on my face and go inside and kiss my wife. This sets the tone for a joyful evening. After all, "the joy of the Lord is my strength" (Nehemiah 8:10).

For my wife and I, we find ways to laugh by playing board games. We put on good music, maybe make a drink, and break out a simple game. If we're not in the mood for a board game, we toss on a pot of decaf coffee, sit at the kitchen table, and share stories about our day. Just being with each other and sharing stories makes us laugh and brings us joy. Especially if we're fighting or having a bad day, forcing ourselves to laugh is good medicine. It's amazing how disarming a laugh can be when you are at war with your spouse.

It is quite easy after a long day to just sit in front of the TV and check out. There is nothing wrong with that on some nights, but I would say if you are doing that every night, you may want to ask if it is good for your relationship.

Pray Together: I don't know why it is so hard to pray with my spouse, but it is. It's almost like there is some kind of spiritual darkness that doesn't want us unified before God almighty. I can pray with my friends and with strangers at church, but my wife and I have a hard time praying with each other. Sure, I pray on my own and she prays on her own, but rarely together.

The crazy thing is that when we pray together, we become more unified than ever. We can feel the power of the Lord between us. "Where two or more are gathered, there the Lord is" (Matthew 18:20). Find a good time for the two of you to pray together. Pray for each other, your marriage, your kids, and anything else that is on your heart. For us, we pray best in the morning before the kids get up and the day gets going. Find your time to join with your spouse to commune with the Lord through prayer.

Serve Your Spouse: Sometimes the best thing I can do for my spouse is to serve her. Whether it is doing the dishes, running an errand, or folding the laundry, I can love my wife well by lightening her load. We discuss who is doing what, so we have clear expectations. "Serve well, as Jesus came to serve, not to be served" (see Matthew 20:28).

My wife knows I hate taking out the trash, so she kindly takes on that duty. I know she doesn't like emptying the dishwasher, so I do that for her. We don't keep a tally of who does what or get mad when the other doesn't do as much as the other. Instead, we give grace, knowing that sometimes life is hard and the other one could use a break.

A chore chart has helped us immensely and clearly defines "who does what." Is it childish to have a chore chart as a grown man? Yes. Yes, it is. But you can call me childish all day long if it means I'm loving my wife by serving her well.

Be Intentional: Everyone likes it when someone else goes out of their way to make them feel special—seen and known. Your spouse is no different. This doesn't mean you have to spend a ton of money or be extravagant. It just means to do things that let the other person know you care about them. A little intentionality goes a long way to show your spouse that you love them.

For my wife and I, we do two things: date nights and trips together. We know the importance of getting away, just the two of us, on a consistent basis. My wife also likes it when I plan and do something special for her. She loves adventures, so I do my best to do something new for her every so often.

On date nights, we get dressed up, go to dinner, and truly catch up with each other. We get out of town for a couple of days at least once a quarter. There, we make memories, rest, and experience a new environment. This doesn't have to break the bank either. We have been camping, to friends' lake houses, and to someone's trailer in the middle of nowhere. Just getting out of your normal environment can do wonders for your marriage.

Become an Expert: Learn as much as you can about how your spouse is wired. My wife knows that I am an extrovert and a visionary and that I like the finer things in life. I know my wife loves adventure and creativity and needs her alone time. Taking personality tests and finding our love language has also helped us love each other in the right ways.

Give Space: In my first few years of marriage, I always wanted to spend time with my wife to the detriment of spending time with my friends. I did that because that's what I thought a good husband did.

One day, a friend of mine called and asked me to play basketball.

"I can't. I'm hanging out with my wife tonight," I said.

My wife pulled me aside. "Why don't you go play basketball? You love basketball and hanging out with friends. I'll stay here and take a bath. I love and need my alone time."

That's the night that I figured out my wife doesn't have the same needs as I do. I need people, and she needs alone time. I can go out and she can rest, and we both come back recharged. That's a win-win. What brings your spouse life? What makes them come alive? Give them the space to do that and, when they return, they will be filled up with life and the energy needed to love you well.

Be the Champion: For a long time into our marriage, I thought marriage was all about dying to self. But isn't there more to marriage? That's when I realized that, instead of focusing on dying to myself, I could focus on championing my wife. I could focus all my strength on helping her become her best self and she would do the same. When you champion your spouse, you help them become all the Lord has and they do the same for you. Although these look similar in action, "helping them become their best self" is a much more encouraging mindset than "dying to self" day after day. Simply put, you'll go a lot further in your marriage by telling your wife what she's doing right instead of focusing on what they are doing wrong.

Pursue Counseling: Sometimes in marriage, you hit some rocky roads that are hard to navigate. In times like these, you may need a guide to help you overcome. It's not *if* you'll need marital counseling, it's *when*. My wife and I have been through some hard times and counseling has helped us learn how to deal with setbacks and unfortunate situations in a healthy, positive way. I know some people, especially guys, may not be open to counseling, but I have found it to be well worth the cost. People spend money on guides and wise counsel to help them eat healthy, exercise, and excel at work. Isn't your marriage just as, if not more, important than all those things? Do your research and be selective about the counselor you choose, and if you can, go with someone endorsed by a trusted leader or pastor.

Have a Healthy Sex Life: Having a healthy sex life is good for several reasons. First, it brings us closer together. Next, it helps me, as a man, stay focused on the love of my life and center my affections on my wife. Lastly, it's fun and gives us both something to look forward to. Sex is a gift from the Lord to be between husband and wife. Celebrate the good gift that it is.

All that being said, I'm amazed at how hard it is to get this one right. Never in a million years would I have thought I would pass up sex, but it gets really tempting when you've had a hard day and all you want to do is go to sleep. Toss in kids, health issues, fighting, and just plain laziness and you've got yourself some issues.

One thing is for certain, talking about sexual expectations helps a ton. Scheduling it and being proactive in pursuing her also can be a good idea. Oftentimes, my wife and I find ourselves "choosing" to have sex than "feeling excited" to have sex. But it always brings us closer together, and that's a good thing.

Don't Give Advice: Often, whether out of fear or pride, I want to give my wife advice and direction as to what she should do with her life. Let me tell you, it has never worked out well. No one likes the advice monster. But then I learned perhaps the most important thing in my marriage: The Lord loves my wife more than I do. He wants her to succeed more than I do, and He has a plan for her life.

My job as a husband is to pray, serve, love, and champion my wife, not give her unsolicited advice. This takes a lot of trust as I must have faith that my wife will consult the Lord, wise counsel, and her friends. I also trust that she will consider me, our family, and our marriage in all the decisions she makes. Instead of telling her what I think, I will pray with her, listen to her process, and ask her questions. But ultimately, she has her own life to live, and God has good things in store for her.

For Your Children

As a father, my children will be influenced by who I am. My character will shape theirs. If I want them to be kind, I must be kind. They will learn how to forgive by watching me forgive those who hurt me. If I want my kids to become something, I must first become that thing. I cannot give to my children what I don't have. If you want your children to love Jesus and love their neighbors well, it starts with you first.

Besides loving my wife well, the other most important and impactful thing I have ever done for my kids is to be around fathers I wanted to be like. If I saw a man who I considered a good father, I would ask him out for coffee and learn from him. Most of these guys learned how to be a good father because they had a good father and/or healthy father figures in their lives.

Date Your Kids: My good friend Bryant taught me to get quality one-on-one time with your kids at least once a week. "Take each one to breakfast once a week," he told me. I started that tradition a few years ago and now Daddy Dates are my kids' favorite events of the week.

During our breakfast, we have no agenda other than spending time with each other. We talk about what they want to talk about, and we eat what they want to eat. Usually, this takes 45 minutes. Every week, when asked what their favorite time of the week was, our kids answer, "My date with Dad."

Although we may not talk about anything important during our breakfasts now, I am laying the foundation for opportunities for serious talks later. When my son is in junior high or high school and something big pops up, he has an opportunity to share it with Dad in a one-on-one setting. He knows he will have Dad's full attention one morning a week for an hour. It is here that I can listen, encourage, and affirm my children. I believe when they are old and think back to their childhood, dates with Dad will be one of the first things they remember.

Make Memories: In preparation for this book, I asked 100 people in my community what they remember most about their childhood. Every single person, without exception, mentioned a memory they had with their dad. Most talked a whole lot more about experiences they had with their father instead of lectures of advice. That struck a chord with me. Typically, I like to rest and chill a lot more than I like to create adventures and experiences. But now it's time to put a little more effort into making memories for my children.

I live in Texas where it is hot and humid about ninety-two percent of the year. But this past winter, we had about a foot of snow dump on us seemingly out of nowhere. I cannot stand the snow. It was a freezing, icy, and miserable week for this warm-blooded Texas boy. The only thing I wanted to do was sit by my fire and read a book with a cup of coffee in my hand. But I remembered the importance of making memories and saw this snowy week as an opportunity for something my kids will talk about when they are adults. So, I bundled up, tied a couple of laundry baskets to the back of my pickup truck, and dragged my kids around the neighborhood. My kids had the time of their lives! We made a memory they will never forget. We created an experience that will outlast my life and bring a smile to my children's faces when they think of it.

So, go the extra mile to create memories for your kids. Get off the couch and get intentional. Making memories will speak volumes about your love for your children. Doing so will give them something they can hold on to that can never be taken away from them.

Go on Family Vacations: In the same vein as making memories, taking a family vacation each year will be something your children always remember. Now, this is especially hard for me as the logical side of me wants to save money and thinks spending money at a waterpark or hotel isn't the best use. It is so worth it though. You don't have to spend a lot of money to do this, as a staycation or camping works just as well as a Hawaii getaway. Just be intentional about unplugging from work and your environment to take a week to just be with your family. They will thank you when they are older. I promise you that.

Provide Loving Discipline: One of my biggest fears as a parent was that disciplining my child would cause them to dislike me. What I have found is the exact opposite; disciplining my children somehow brings us closer together. It is a form of love, as God the Father disciplines those whom He loves (Proverbs 3:12). My rule of thumb is, "Don't let your kids do anything that is unbiblical or will cause you to dislike them." Discipline is correction. Disciplining in love, without anger or raising your voice, is the tricky but important part. Your actions are saying, "You are doing something that is going to cause you harm in the future. Do this instead." Still, it is our job as parents to prepare our children for life, not to be their best friends. The Bible notes that, "No discipline seems pleasant at the time, but painful. Later on, however, it produces a harvest of righteousness and peace for those who have been trained by it" (Hebrews 12:11).

<u>Speak Life Over Your Children:</u> I believe encouraging words can build a person up and help them do the hard things in life. I want my kids to speak life over themselves and learn who the Lord says they are. I want them to walk in wisdom. I believe this will strengthen them as they grow up and help defeat the lies of the enemy. Here's how we do it:

Every morning I take my kids to school. On the car ride there, we play a little game. Here's how it goes. I say the first part of the sentence and they say the second part:

We do the right thing...no matter what.
Why do we fall down? To get back up.
Why do we fail? We learn from our mistakes.
If it's worth doing....it's worth doing right.
Failing...helps you get better.
Life is all about...making good choices over and over again.
If you see something that needs to be done...do it!
Good things happen...when you try new things.
It takes a long time to build trust...and a second to lose it.
You spell faith....R-I-S-K.

It feels good...to make people feel good.
Why do we work hard? To give ourselves the best chance of success.
If we don't know the answer....figure it out. If we can't figure it out....
we ask for help.
What's our people goal? To make their day better.
What's our heart goal? To love all people.
What's our mind goal? To learn something new.
True significance...is making others better.
What do we focus on? Good things, not bad things.
I love you...just as I am.
My character is more important...than what I do.
What do we pursue? Wisdom, knowledge, and understanding.
Life is not fair... Make the best out of what life gives you.
Friends are important....but family is the most important.
It's not...about me!
I am not...what I have.
I am not...what I do.
I am not...what other people think or say about me.
I am...a beloved child of God and that's enough.

Once we're done, I pray for them and I have one of them pray for me.

I'm amazed at how much my kids love this tradition. I have also caught them saying it in the middle of the day and at school. Much to my surprise, my four-year-old daughter knows most of these by heart.

My goal in this is to saturate their hearts with wisdom. I hope they remember these sayings and our car rides all the days of their lives.

<u>Create a Culture of Honor:</u> One thing that we have done in our house is to implement a culture of honor. This means nothing negative is spoken in our house at all times. If you don't like dinner, keep quiet. If someone annoys you, think of something positive to

say. No complaining, no gossiping, nothing disrespectful or hateful is spoken. Only honor. My wife and I believe that if our kids see us being positive and honoring, that will trickle down to them as well. Kids are watching and listening to what we do and say, and how we say it. More is caught than taught and we hope that our kids catch our intentionality in creating a culture of honor.

Let's make positivity, thankfulness, and encouragement the norm. Let's create children who use their words to build up instead of tear down.

Eat Dinner Together: When my parents split up, we stopped having dinner together. As a child, this didn't seem like a big deal. But as I look back on it, it took away the one time during the day when everyone came together and spent time together. We all get busy, but dinner can be the one time you stop and come together as a family. Friends have told me, "My family ate dinner together every single night. No exception." What a cool thing to be able to say about a family!

At our dinner table, we play a simple game of high/low, where we share the high point of our day and the low point of our day. We also share one thing we are thankful for, as this helps keep thanksgiving a priority in our home. On Friday nights, we have pizza and watch a movie. On Saturday nights, we invite a family over for dinner. Obviously, things come up from time to time and you can't eat together as a whole family. But making dinner a priority can be a healthy tradition for any family. It is a good time to catch up on what everyone is up to, encourage, and celebrate each other.

Serve Together: I have a friend in Dallas who runs a homeless shelter. One day, we were having coffee and I asked him, "How did you get so passionate about serving the homeless?" He answered, "I had a great family growing up. I never went without. I guess I first became passionate about serving the homeless as a kid. My dad made my family serve at a shelter a few times a year. At first, I hated it, but then the Lord did something in my heart toward the homeless. That put me on the path to get to where I am today."

Serving together is a great way to introduce your kids to the importance of serving others. Expose them to people who have different circumstances than you do, and help them get their eyes off themselves and to grow in selflessness. A service project a month can be a good thing for a family. Plus, you never know what the Lord will do with your children when you teach them different ways to impact the Kingdom.

Enter Into Their World: I have a friend whose teenage son is obsessed with video games. It's the only thing in the world that he cares or talks about. This father was having a hard time with this because he didn't have a high view of video games and or think they were a smart use of time.

One day, this father felt compelled to enter his son's world when the Lord placed on his heart that, "People feel loved when you love what they love." Instead of telling his son to turn off the video game, he sat down and started playing with him. For hours, they sat and played video games together. While it wasn't the most productive use of their time, at least the father was getting time with his son. They continued playing together daily.

One day, the son opened up about his life in the middle of a video game. They hit pause and had what my friend would consider to be the most productive conversation they'd ever had together. And all because he made an effort to enter his son's world and love what his son loved. That communicated more than any words could to that young man.

What does your kid love and how can you enter into that with them? Whether it is basketball, art, or dancing, love what your kid loves. Your presence alone will earn you the right to be heard. Kids don't care what you know until they know that you care. Leaving your world and entering theirs is a great way to let them know that you care about them and want to be with them.

Set Healthy Boundaries at Work: As someone who didn't have much as a child, my desire to give my kids everything they could possibly want is a temptation to me. I want them to go to the finest Christian private school, live in the biggest house, and have everything I didn't have as a child. The only problem with that is all those things cost money and, for me, providing those things means working longer and harder to make more money. And that means time away from my family.

I have a lot of friends who have come from wealth and they all tell me, "I would have traded in the big house, nice school, and quality summer camps to just spend more time with my dad." Let that sink in for a moment.

The enemy hates family and will do whatever he can to break the family apart. If he can get you to work long hours, for whatever reason, so you don't spend time with your wife and kids, he's won.

Work hard and provide for your family, but trust that the Lord will take care of your every need. God knows what you need and He will provide for you. Make every attempt to set healthy boundaries regarding work. For me, it is dates with my kids three mornings a week and home by six o'clock each night. I don't bring my computer home and I don't have work apps on my phone. This way, I can be fully present at home. It may seem inconvenient and extreme now, but I promise your children will reap the benefits of your presence.

Tell Me...

- Which one of the topics above caught your attention the most?
- What do you want your children or future children to say about their dad when they are adults? How can you start becoming that today?
- How can you avoid the trap of losing your sense of priorities and neglecting the very things that matter most?

CHAPTER 23

Become the Guide

THERE WAS A time in my life when I would have said growing up without a father was the worst thing that could have happened to me. I just couldn't comprehend why the Lord would allow something like this to happen.

One thing that is so difficult in following the Lord is the fact that often His ways do not make sense. The Bible even says that what was meant to kill you, can actually turn out to be used for good (see Genesis 50:20). I guess that is why faith is such an important concept in our relationship with God. Most of the time I find myself saying, "I don't understand this God, but I trust that You know what You're doing and that You are good."

Growing up without a father in the home can produce anger, frustration, and bitterness in you, or it can give you the opportunity to endure hardships, have joy despite circumstances, and forgive those who have hurt you. People who have issues with their father have the choice to believe that God is good and knows what He's doing, or they can choose to believe that God cannot redeem the situation.

I know "choosing God" in these situations seems simple, but simple isn't always easy. In fact, choosing to believe that God is good despite circumstances and not allowing bitterness and anger to ruin my relationship with God is one of the hardest things I've ever done...and it took me a really long time to get there. One thing I know for certain, there is no way I would have stayed in the game to see God's faithfulness without the help of a few people.

So many people have helped me in the healing process of my past and guided me into the man that I am today. I am where I am today because of pastors, businessmen, mentors, and friends. Each had a unique and important role in helping me heal from my past. Now, it is my joy and pleasure to get to do the same for others who find themselves in the very situation that I once found myself in. What an incredible opportunity I have to help others find the freedom that I now experience.

You have the same opportunity.

We have the chance to give away what we have received. Healing and freedom were never meant to stop with us but are tools that we can put in our toolbelt to help others experience the goodness of God the Father.

Now that you have experienced freedom yourself, God can use your testimony to help others start the healing journey in their own lives. Go and make disciples, helping others experience the freedom that Christ has to offer.

Here is how to start the process of helping others heal from their father wound.

Help Them Identify Their Wound

When meeting men for the first time, I always like to see if the Lord can use me to minister to them in some way. This isn't a burden or a task that needs to be done; instead, it is a joy to try to be a light wherever I go. I always ask the Lord to use me if He sees fit. That being said, I have found *three* ways in which the Lord can use you to help others identify their need for healing in their relationship with their father. They include: leading with your testimony, being curious by asking good questions, and being a listening ear.

Once you've experienced the healing journey yourself, you will start to see others who could benefit from that same journey. You can pick it up when they talk about their past or their family. Easy questions to find out where they stand with their father include:

- What was your childhood like?
- Would you say that you are pretty close with your parents?
- Can you tell me about your father?

If you find them talking at length about their family, but only speaking of their mother, you may be on to something.

When I find myself in situations where I can pick up on the fact that the person I am talking to may come from a difficult past, I simply try to naturally incorporate my testimony into conversation with them. I don't try to force it and I don't keep talking about it if they don't seem interested in hearing it. However, I do pray for an opportunity to talk about the healing journey that the Lord brought me on and how much freedom I have received from dealing with my past.

I know that it is not my responsibility to "fix" this person, but I also want to see if the Lord opens a door for me to share about His goodness. It's not my responsibility to make sure someone deals with their past. It is my responsibility to share what He's done in my life. There is power in our testimony.

Sometimes I can share my testimony by asking questions like:

- "What are you passionate about?" Once they tell me what they are passionate about, they will probably want to know what I'm passionate about. This opens the door to sharing about my passion for helping others experience what I experienced.

- "Have you read anything good lately?" Knowing they will probably ask me the same question gives me a chance to talk about a book that helped me in my freedom journey.

I can also share when talking about fathering with any other fathers. There is always a chance to ask a question like, "Did you ever do this with your dad?" which could open up a conversation about their relationship with their father.

I have different versions of my testimony. I have the one-minute testimony, which is short and simple. Next is the three-minute testimony, which adds a little more detail about my story. Lastly, is the longer eight to ten-minute-long testimony, which tells my whole story. Here, you probably want to stick to the one or three-minute-long testimony. You will have the opportunity to share the longer one if you can tell they have an appetite for it.

I'll be the first to say that most men do not open up easily about these things, but every so often you will find one who is really interested in learning more about the healing journey. You can tell they are interested by the look in their eye and the attention they give you when you share your testimony. If they respond with a "Cool, man," you should probably take the hint and stop sharing with him. If they respond with questions of their own or if they share that they can relate, you can continue the conversation. Your testimony paves the way for them to share their own.

If the conversation progresses, I have found the best thing you can do is to be a listening ear. For most men, this isn't a topic they talk about often, and being vulnerable about their past is very difficult. You can show empathy by using phrases like, "I can relate to that," or, "I know what that feels like," but try to let them talk as much as possible.

Once you feel like the conversation is at a stopping point, I always give them the opportunity to connect further. I try to exchange contact information and let them know that I am happy to go out to coffee or lunch to continue the discussion. If I feel like I made a connection with them, I even will send them a text or give them a call a day or two after we met just to allow them to chat more.

If that happens, they will almost always come with questions about your journey. Since it is impossible to lead someone to a place where you have not gone, this is a fantastic chance to use your testimony to usher them into their own healing journey.

Usher Them into the Journey of Healing

If you find yourself with a large chunk of time with someone who is interested in learning more about the healing journey, it is often best to share the action plan through your testimony.

Here, you can talk about:

- The power of "going back to go forward" and how your past was keeping you from becoming the person that you wanted to be.
- How forgiving your father and those who wronged you released you from bitterness and anger.
- How you see God, as this has massive implications for your relationship with God, yourself, and others.
- The difference between seeing yourself as an orphan and walking in sonship.
- How to trust the process and rely on God's timing, not our own.
- The importance of surrounding yourself with supportive people who can encourage you during challenging times, celebrate with you during good times, and pick you up when you fall down.

Sharing your experience will give them the confidence they need to possibly start their own journey, but it will also provide them with tools and tips to help them along the way. You can share the things that you got right and what you would do differently if you had the chance. You can talk about the people who helped you along the way and the ones who encouraged you to start the journey in the first place. You can share what you learned and how it is positively impacting you and your relationships today.

There are many ways one can start the journey of healing. Some people find their start at programs such as men's church groups or accountability groups. Others find it at counseling or group therapy, while others prefer finding mentors and coaches. It truly is whatever they feel the most comfortable with and what they believe the Lord is calling them to.

This is where you can serve as the guide to another as they start the healing journey themselves. As a guide, you allow the other person to do most of the work. They pick their final destination and the pace at which they want to go. They are the ones taking the steps and doing the hard work. You are simply there to encourage them when things get hard or to use your experience to offer wisdom when they ask for help.

The power is in the process of the journey of healing. It is a difficult journey to start and an even more difficult one to see through to the end. While you have experience and advice to give the one making the journey, the best thing you can give them is your presence.

Supporting from the Sidelines

I have a few friends who like to run Ironman races. If you are unfamiliar with the Ironman, it is a 2.4-mile swim, followed by a 112-mile bike ride and a 26.2-mile run. All of this happens in one day. I know, it's as crazy as it sounds.

On race days, I have gone out to support my friends, but it doesn't feel like I am supporting them in any major way. I hold up a sign, encourage them when they run past, and maybe give them a little cup of water if they are thirsty. The whole process is short-lived compared to the long journey they are making. It simply doesn't feel like I did much to contribute to their success, but, and this happens all the time, my friend will come find me after the race and say, "Thank you so much for your support. It really helped me a ton. I couldn't have done it without you."

My response is always, "You did all the hard work. I was just on the sidelines cheering you on and supporting you from time to time."

When you encounter someone who wants to start their healing journey, you get to be the person on the sidelines who cheers them on and gives them water when they are a little thirsty. Even better, you know what it's like to endure the journey because you have gone before them and done the journey yourself.

You of all people know just how long and difficult the healing journey can be, but you also know that the journey is well worth your time and effort. Just like any journey that you go on, it is always beneficial to understand what you are getting yourself into before you start the trek.

If you find someone who is interested in starting a healing journey of their own, you get the opportunity to prepare them for the journey before they start. Using your testimony, you can let them know what you experienced so that they can prepare their hearts, avoid missteps, or be better prepared for the road ahead.

More than anything, they just need your presence. Keep up with them. Pursue them. Reach out to them often and set consistent times to meet frequently. The journey is hard, and while your advice and experience are helpful, your encouragement is what will be the most beneficial. Having a listening ear or having someone to talk to can be extremely life-giving. They need their tank filled up, and your presence can be the thing that gives them what they need to keep on going.

And when you see it becoming difficult and you feel the urge to protect your friend to keep them from experiencing discomfort, know that God is working in the process and that He is always up to something. One of the most helpful phrases I tell myself when seeing a friend struggle is, "God loves this person more than I do, and He knows what He's doing."

Releasing control and surrendering others to the Lord's process takes a remarkable amount of faith in the goodness of God. So often we want to keep others from experiencing pain, but what if the pain is exactly what they need to have a breakthrough to true healing? Sometimes, by taking control of the process, we actually get in the way of what the Lord is trying to do. While we want to be helpful, we are actually doing the opposite. This is especially true the closer you are to the one who is embarking on the journey. Those we love the most, we typically try to protect the most. Let's flip the script. Those we love the most, we ought to surrender the most.

While some of us may want to go on the journey with our loved ones, it is their journey to make. Sure, you can guide and help when they need it, but this is a solo, inside job. The best thing you can do is to be there when they need a little support. You can provide blueprints, and you should, but they must pick up the tools and start to build.

Tell Me...

- Is there someone in your life who could benefit from dealing with their relationship with their father?
- Do you feel equipped to usher and guide someone through this journey? Why or why not?
- How do you feel about sharing your father wound journey with others?

CHAPTER 24

Legacy

M Y GRANDMOTHER WAS one of the most important people in my life. In fact, she and my grandfather were like second parents to me. After my grandfather passed and as she grew
older, she developed dementia and we had to place her in a nurs-
ing home for her to receive the care she needed. I'd go see her once
a week to make sure she was doing okay and keep her company. It
was hard to see her in her weakened condition in which she could
hardly communicate. But it was good to be with her no less.

She knew when the end of her life was nearing. She gathered
her family and just wanted to be with us. She couldn't speak, so we
did all the talking. My mom told stories about her growing up. The
grandkids told memories of spending weeks at Grandma's house
during the summer. We talked about chocolate chip cookies and
peach cobbler. We laughed as we remembered my grandfather's
idiosyncrasies and his sly smile. As time went on, we talked about
the Lord and what a dedicated follower of Jesus my grandmother
was. We sang hymns and discussed the Bible. We spoke of the important things in life, of family and faith.

When you are old and nearing the end of your life, what are the things you will care about? When you are lying on your death-bed, will you be talking about things or will you be talking about people? Will your focus be on your bank account or on your char-acter and your legacy? Let those same things be a top priority for you now. Your family, your spouse and kids, and your faith. The Lord can rewrite your story and create in you someone who takes a generational curse and turns it into a generational blessing.

Who will you want around your bed? For me, it is my wife, my children, and maybe a few key family members and friends. We will speak of memories, of love, and of adventures. The only ques-tions I will care about are:

- "Lord Jesus, are you proud of how I lived my life for You?"
- "Is my wife proud of me, and would she marry me again if she had to do it all over again?"
- "Do my sons want to be like me and does my daughter want to marry someone like me?"

What will your obituary say? What kind of stories will peo-ple share at your funeral? Who will be at your funeral? Will they talk about your heart or your accomplishments? Did you make the world a brighter place? Did others experience the love of Jesus through your words and actions?

My final charge to you is to allow God to father you. "Come to me..." Jesus says. "And I will give you rest."

So go to Him. Let God the Father do what He does best. Let go of control and let Him take over. After all, change comes from Him, not necessarily from our efforts.

The journey of allowing God to father you is one of patience, endurance, and perseverance. Give yourself plenty of grace as you take one step at a time. You will fall down, but the Good Shepherd will be there to pick you up. Friends and mentors will be there as you grow in forgiveness and change how you see yourself, God, and others. Whatever you do, don't give up. The lifelong journey will be worth it. Everything you need comes from the Father. It's not reliance on you, but dependence on Him.

Go to the Father. Surround yourself with people who can help you do that. Sit in His presence, and allow yourself to be loved and led by the One who loves you. Daily shed all aspects of your orphan nature and remind yourself that you are a son. Sit at your Father's table. Come as you are.

Healing your father wound is not a one-time action, but a moment-by-moment trek. Some days will be easy. Others will be harder. But you will not be alone.

You may have had to grow up not knowing the love of a father. You may have been alone and hurt by those who should have loved you most. Your story doesn't have to be the story of your children. Your children will never know a day when their father wasn't for them. Your spouse will say that you are the best person they know. Jesus will say, "Well done, good and faithful servant." You can become what you never had.

And it can start today.

Tell Me...

- Picture yourself in your eighties knowing that your time has come. You are nearing the end of your race and you have a few days to reflect upon the life that you lived. Who are you spending your last days with? What are you all talking about?

- Pretend that your time has come and you have finished your race. Who would you like to speak at your funeral? Your spouse? Your children? What would you like for them to say? Take a few moments and write the eulogies that you'd like for your loved ones to read.

CHAPTER 25

The Stages

AS I LOOK back upon my life growing up without a father, I can see now the different stages of my father wound journey. No two stages were the same, and some were harder than others, but all of them were necessary to turn me into the man that I am today. In fact, I am still a work in progress, as new experiences and situations always seem to give me new opportunities to allow my father wound to refine me.

I remember absorbing the stares and the feeling of embarrassment I had walking into school as a twelve-year-old the day after my father left.

I remember in college, being overwhelmed with jealousy and anger at my friend when his dad bought him a new car.

I remember as an adult, a mentor introducing me to his friends and the shame that overcame me when he called me "fatherless."

I remember...

I never want my father wound to define me. I never want it to disqualify me or become my identity. Instead, I view my situation as my very own, unique journey with its own obstacles and challenges. This is the journey that I'm on for a reason that I will never know. The good news is that the Lord can use this obstacle to make me look more like Him, which is indeed the greatest gift He can ever give to me.

I believe James is right when he says, "Consider it pure joy, my brothers and sisters, whenever you face trials of many kinds, because you know that the testing of your faith produces perseverance. Let perseverance finish its work so that you may be mature and complete, not lacking anything" (James 1:2-4). The hard things in life really do turn you into the mature believer that we all want to be. If you let it.

We all have things in life that can be considered a challenge or an obstacle. My mentor Steve Allen has ALS, better known as Lou Gehrig's Disease. It has left him without the ability to do the basic things that people do. That's his mountain to climb. I have friends who deal with alcoholism, financial issues, and job insecurity. I have others who have spent months in the hospital watching their child suffer through sickness. Hurts happen. Families go through loss and pain.

The older I get, the more I realize that this world truly is a broken place. The statement, "In this world, you will have trouble" (John 16:33) gets more real day by day. No one has it easy. This thing called life gets the best of all of us from time to time.

But this is my journey. The obstacle that I must overcome. And on this journey, I have found that one must go through certain stages to make progress on the trek.

If you are going through your own journey, or possibly guiding someone through their own, here are a few stages that you can be on the lookout for. Whether you have gone through these stages already or will be approaching them soon, I pray they are helpful for you as you continue ahead.

Curiosity Stage

Don Tope is a legend in the eyes of me and my high school friends. The mere mention of the word "Don" will make all of us smile and respond with a story or two. That's because Don was the only example of a father to our entire friend group. Don would take us camping, grill us steaks, and fill us up with encouragement every time we saw him. He worked on cars, snuck a cigar every so often, and had a goatee. He was a man's man, and we all looked up to him. And while I am beyond thankful for "The Don's" role in my life, his fatherly presence always made me ask a few questions in the back of my mind.

"I wonder why I don't have a father around?"

"Was it my fault?"

"Why doesn't my dad want to be around me?"

"Why am I different from all the other kids?"

This is the curiosity stage. The stage in which a child begins to come up with his own narrative as to why his dad is not around. Most of the time, the disappearance of a child's father is shrouded in mystery. That's understandable, as I wasn't ready to hear all the details of my parent's divorce. But the enemy can use the cloak of mystery to cloud my thinking with a lot of lies as to why my dad isn't around anymore. This is a prime time for Satan to start lying, often in the form of a question. He finds a vulnerable child without a dad around and he starts bombarding the kid with lies. Lies that oftentimes make the child believe that the absence of his father was somehow related to something he did. It was his fault. He's to blame. And that's never a good thing. The feeling of fault can lead us into the next stage of the father-wound journey.

High Emotion Stage

"Forget him. I don't want anything to do with that guy."

The feeling of abandonment and the weight that it was probably somehow your fault, mixed with the strong feelings of adolescence can produce what we like to call the "Anger, Apathy, or Prove It" stage of the father-wound journey. It is in this stage, which typically begins during adolescence, where the following phrases may be uttered:

"I hate my father, and I'm glad he's not around"

"I don't have anything to offer, so what use is it trying?"

"My dad doesn't care about me. I doubt anyone truly does."

"I'm going to prove to people that I'm a manly man."

Let me break down how anger, apathy, and the need to prove myself played out in my life.

The anger produced by my relationship with my father kept me from talking to him consistently for over a decade. My anger not only negatively impacted me but those that were closest to me, as they often got the brunt of my outbursts.

The feeling of insecurity and fear led me to hide in apathy for a lot of my teenage years. I didn't go to prom because "Why would anyone want to date me?" At times, I didn't try out for sports or pursue my interests because I knew that I would fail. There's no use in taking risks when you know how it's going to turn out.

Proving that I had what it took to succeed turned out to be a very dangerous endeavor for me. Whether it was drinking a near-toxic level of alcohol to show my friends I was a real man or almost getting into fights to prove my toughness, I simply thought I had to do incredibly stupid things to get people to respect me, like me, and keep me around.

This stage taught me how to suppress my emotions and pretend like all was okay. It also produced many times when those suppressed emotions exploded and created a lot of chaos in my life. The bad news about this stage is the fact that you can stay here for a long time. It will not go away until you decide it's time to change, and usually, that is one rough wake-up call.

Whether it is living life in the fast lane, handling emotional blow-ups, or hiding in your room, it's only a matter of time before you look yourself in the mirror and say, "I'm not sure I like this person. There has got to be more to life than this." This realization can lead us to the next stage.

Desire Stage

Sometimes there is a moment in a person's life that causes them to make drastic changes. For me, it was when I had tried absolutely everything to make me happy and nothing did the trick. For one of my friends, it was a car wreck that almost took his life. For another, it was almost missing the birth of his son because he refused to cancel a work meeting that could have gotten him the deal of his life. Whatever the reason, there are times when you seem to wake up and say, "Something has to change."

Enter the *desire stage*. It is at this stage that you may say:

"I'm done flying solo. I want to learn everything that it takes to be a godly, positive man by submitting to and building relationships with older, father-figures."

"I don't want what happened to me to happen to my kids. Something has to change, and that change starts with me."

"I want to be the best husband and father I can be. I want to be like other, healthy people and become what I never had."

This stage is one of the more exciting stages because, for some, you see someone realizing that change is possible, maybe for the first time in their entire life. Change can happen quickly as they learn a few key lessons that can accelerate the healing process.

First off, they start to see the impact of who they hang out with. The decision to start surrounding themselves with godly people who encourage them to be the best version of themselves starts to pay dividends. Next, they get the courage to ask an older man to mentor them, disciple them, or invest in their life. They soak up all that they learn, maybe because they are starting to see some fruit from their labor. It's almost like a lightbulb goes off as they realize,

"If I just follow what these mentors say and do what the Bible tells me to do, things tend to go better!"

Lastly, they grow a self-starter mentality, breaking free of the bondage of apathy and insecurity. Sure, you still fall down, but you are quick to get back up and you do not quit. The foundation of a transformed life starts to form as they embrace the humility to heed advice and the courage to take action.

People start to say, "There's something different about them" and, "They've changed, for the better." This is the beginning of something good. But like most difficult journeys, just when you thought it was getting easy, you encounter the hardest hill yet.

The Forgiveness Stage

While we've looked at this topic in detail elsewhere, it's worth mentioning here again briefly. There is no going around the wound that was produced by your father. You must go right through it. Forgiving your father may very well be one of the most difficult things that you will ever experience, but the freedom it produces is very much worth it.

The beginning of this stage can sound something like:

"I want to get rid of this anger in my heart. I want to be obedient to God and trust His way is better."

"I realize forgiveness is more about me than it is about my father."

That's when the practical steps come into play. First, you recruit a shepherd to guide you through this. This is someone who you trust and who can encourage you to keep going when the going gets tough. This person can also help with the next step: identifying the ways his hurt is limiting or harming you. This will almost always cause certain emotions to pop up, and we must deal with those in a safe and effective way. Doing that requires that we muster up the courage to deal with past hurts and disappointments.

True forgiveness almost always follows this pattern:
- Desire to forgive comes first
- Words of forgiveness come second
- Truly forgiving with your whole heart is the last step

All three of these actions must be completed in order to achieve lasting change. If possible, meet in person to voice forgiveness. Phone calls and letters work as well if a meeting isn't an option.

This stage is almost always the most difficult, but once it is finished, it should catapult you into the last stage, which also happens to be the most exciting stage.

Identity Stage

The last stage is where you say, "I want to learn how to be a son of God and come to accept the love of a father who will never leave me. I want life and life to the fullest." Sometimes your change is obvious and a one-time event, but for me, it was a slow change.

One day I realized that my temper was almost non-existent, and I had a whole lot more joy and compassion for others. The patience came slowly as I was able to keep my cool in almost any situation. It was easier for me to give grace and forgive others. My wife and kids said that I was a blessing in their life.

"My dear Lord. It's happening," I said to myself with a smile on my face.

This is hopefully the stage that you will live from for the rest of your days. Of course, there will be some days when you forget who you are and slip back into old thinking patterns. I'm not perfect, and I still yell at my kids from time to time. But most days are lived out with my eyes on my Heavenly Father and advancing His Kingdom for His glory. Many days I have a peace that passes all understanding.

The symptoms of this stage include:

- Leaving the orphan mindset and adopting a mindset of sonship
- Ability to serve others because you are confident the Lord will take care of you
- Ability to take risks, forgive, trust, give and receive love, etc...
- Becoming what you never had, dissolving a generational curse, and creating a generational blessing

The stages of your father wound may look very similar to these or they may not. Every person is different, and every stage looks different depending on your story. Some stages may be short, while others may last a long time. In some ways, we are always in some part of each stage. I still think about my childhood and struggle from time to time with apathy and anger. I still desire to grow in certain areas and new experiences bring up new areas for me to forgive. Walking in my identity as a son is an everyday battle.

It is my prayer that seeing these stages will give you confidence to know that you are not alone on this journey. My hope is that it gives you the confidence to endure and persevere through whatever the enemy may toss your way.

Freedom is near. And I, for one, believe that you can do it. Onward.

Tell Me:

- What stage do you find yourself in currently? What obstacles have you found on your journey?
- Can you relate to the quotes used in each stage? If so, please describe how those played out in your life.
- What do you think when you read James 1:2-4? In what ways have you seen the trials that you have experienced produce opportunities to grow in maturity?

ACKNOWLEDGEMENTS

To the men who have invested in me at some point in my life, I thank you. Some have invested a little, while others have invested a lot. Some have invested spiritually or professionally, while others have invested financially. Regardless, God has used it all. In no specific order, I'd like to thank Fred Henninghausen, Mark Malcolm, Don Tope, Aaron Andress, Bob Strader, Dan Niederhofer, Randy Larson, Joel Busby, Paul Gittemeier, Alex Louis, Bob Williams, John Bower, John Kaserman, Joshua Flynt, Steve Allen, Don Finto, Bob Eagle, Mark Anthony, Kyle Martin, Bryant Gullette, Mac Macfarlan, Scott Frost, John Williams, and Pat Murphy.

Writing a book is a long and arduous process. I am thankful to Nick Poe, Mick Murray, and Craig Cunningham for helping make this book happen.

I am beyond thankful for my friends who have walked closely with me during this season of life. Thank you especially to Ben DuBose, Michael Boone, Alex Eagle, Jeremy Sain, Taylor Vieger, and John Barnard. Also, thank you to Roundtable One, Miller Time, and the Ten Thousand Fathers.

To my beautiful children Zach Jr., Stephen, and Joanna. It is my joy to be your father. I know I don't always get it right, but I pray and hope I am a tremendous blessing in your life. I can't wait to watch you become all that the Lord has for you. I believe in you.

To both my mom and dad: My goal was to tell my perspective of my story that both helped people and honored you two. I hope and pray I accomplished that. I know our story isn't perfect, but I am thankful for you two and I love you, even if I am not the best at showing it.

To my beautiful wife, Sara. Thank you for everything. There is no one else I'd want to go on this crazy adventure with than you. I love you.

Lastly, thank You, Jesus. For everything. Thank You for Your faithfulness and for being a perfect Father. I am grateful and humbled. Here's to more of You.

MAN OF GOD

I am a man of God.

I am strong, fearless, and courageous. I walk in wisdom and power.

I can do hard things
and I get up when I fall down.

I was created on purpose for a purpose. I will do the right thing no matter what. I'm a hard worker who does my best. I am loved and will love others with the love of Jesus. I will forgive because I am forgiven. I know the Holy Spirit is with me AND WILL LEAD ME.

I live life to the fullest because I know God is a good father who I can trust.

I am a world changer and a history maker. I am a man of God.

DAUGHTER OF THE KING

I am a daughter of the King.

I am beautiful inside and out.

I am full of strength, worth, and value.

I can do hard things and I get up when I fall down.

I was created on purpose for a purpose. I will do the right thing no matter what.

I am a hard worker who does my best.

I am loved and will love others with the love of Jesus. I will forgive because I am forgiven.

I know the Holy Spirit is with me and will lead me.

I live life to the fullest because I know God is a good father who I can trust.

I am a world changer and a history maker. I am a daughter of the King.

KID SAYINGS

We do the right thing... no matter what.

Why do we fall down? To get back up.

Why do we fail? We learn from our mistakes.

If it's worth doing, it's worth doing right.

Failing helps you get better.

Life is all about... making good choices over and over again.

If you see something that needs to be done... do it!

Good things happen...when you try new things.

It takes a long time to build trust, and a second to loose it.

You spell faith R-I-S-K.

It feels good... to make people feel good.

Why do we work hard? To give ourself the best chance of success.

If we don't know the answer, figure it out. If we can't figure it out, we ask for help.

True significance... is making others better.

What do we focus on? Good things, not bad things.

I love you... just as I am.

My character is more important... than what I do.

What do we pursue? Wisdom, knowledge and understanding.

What's our people goal? To make their day better.

What's our heart goal? To love all people.

What's our mind goal? To learn something new.

Don't be afraid ... to be your true, authentic self.

Go after... what gives you joy.

If you want nice things... you have to work hard and take care of them.

If you don't quit... you win.

Life is not fair. Make the best out of what life gives you.

Friends are important, but family is the most important.

Be nice to everyone... you never know how God will use them.

Get good at... asking really good questions.

Make new friends.

Faithful with the little. Master over much.

It's not... about me!

I am not what I have.

I am not what I do.

I am not what other people think or say about me.

I am a beloved son of God and that's enough.

ZACH GARZA is passionate about relationships because the Lord used relationships to change his life. He has been a part of multiple mentoring non-profit organizations and now focuses his time on helping others in the realm of mentoring, discipleship, and fathering.

His days are spent investing in servant-leaders who invest in others. His joy is to add value through guiding others to overcome their obstacles and encouraging them to see themselves how God sees them.

Zach and his wife Sara live in Waco, Texas with their three children Zach Jr., Stephen, and Joanna. He loves spending time with his family, playing basketball, and eating tacos. Zach is also a keynote speaker for ministries and non-profits and would be honored to help you in any way that he can.

Learn more at:

www.YouCanMentor.com *and* www.RaisingUpFathers.com

or you can contact him at:

Zach@YouCanMentor.com

Endnotes

1   No Longer Fatherless. *Statistics on Fatherlessness in America and the Profound Impact of Mentoring.* (Blog, 2010). https://www.nolongerfatherless.org/statistics#:~:text=Here%20are%20some%20troubling%20statistics,children%20are%20from%20fatherless%20homes

2   Family History and Alcohol Abuse." Los Angeles County Department of Mental Health. Accessed November, 2023. https://dmh.lacounty.gov/our-services/employment-education/education/alcohol-abuse-faq/family-history/.

3   Epstein, Sarah, LMFT. *What Is a Cycle-Breaker?* Psychology Today. July 15, 2022. https://www.psychologytoday.com/us/blog/between-the-generations/202207/what-is-cycle-breaker.

4   Ronin, Kara. "How to Not Waste the First 7 Seconds of a First Impression." Executive Impressions, March 2, 2015. https://www.executive-impressions.com/blog/not-waste-7-seconds-first-impression.

5   Ebstein, Jill. "The Challenge of First Impressions." My Journal Courier, August 12, 2023. https://www.myjournalcourier.com/opinion/article/commentary-18284968.php.

6   Cloud, Henry, and John Townsend. 1992. Boundaries: When to Say Yes, How to Say No To Take Control of Your Life. Grand Rapids, MI: Zondervan.